Angels Are Among Us

Foundational Scriptures:
Psalm 103:20–22;
Hebrews 1–13:2:1–9

Are There Angels Among Us?

TIMOTHY R WILLIAMS

ISBN 979-8-88685-734-4 (paperback)
ISBN 979-8-88832-432-5 (hardcover)
ISBN 979-8-88685-735-1 (digital)

Christian Faith Publishing
832 Park Avenue
Meadville, PA 16335
www.christianfaithpublishing.com

Printed in the United States of America

DEDICATION

Special thanks to my wife, Tammy, my three children and their spouses, and my nine grandchildren who allow me to travel to the nations to share the good news of Jesus Christ. To all my ministry supporters who pray and give so that I may go to the nations. Special thanks to my daughter-in-law Callie who proofread and helped with the manuscript for this book.

CONTENTS

Introduction vii

Chapter 1:   General Information about Angels 1

Chapter 2:   Angels, Man, and Jesus....................................25

Chapter 3:   Three Heavens 39

Chapter 4:   Organization and Classification of Angels 42

Chapter 5:   Lucifer/Satan..62

Chapter 6:   Fallen Angels/Demons......................................70

Chapter 7:   Spiritual Warfare 78

Chapter 8:   Healing and Angels 85

Chapter 9:   Activating Angels...89

Chapter 10: Can a Christian Be Demon Possessed?....................105

Chapter 11: The Truth about Angels.....................................120

Chapter 12: Bible Stories Concerning Angels and Their Benefit 122

Chapter 13: Topical Index for "Angel" 127

Chapter 14: Bible Scriptures Concerning Angels........................132

INTRODUCTION

This book is an accumulation of information from courses taken while attending two different Bible schools. Some text and information came from reading thirteen different books and numerous articles concerning the topic of angels, demons, and heaven's messengers. Scriptures are from the NKJV, unless noted differently. This is by no means an exhausted study of angels. I have tried to share the things I believe to be important that will help to ensure we live a victorious life. Angels are more of a part of our daily lives than most people realize, including Christians. Hopefully, this book will help you to expect and believe that angels are among us. They are here to help with our callings and ministries, just as they are here to protect, bring messages, and work on our behalf. Angels have been given charge over you and me. Each angel has been given assignments to carry out according to God's Word. Mark Hankins said, "God's Word was spoken so it could be written, so it could be spoken." Angels hearken to God's Word and His commandments. My focus for this book is to show there are angels among us.

CHAPTER 1

General Information about Angels

Foundational Scriptures: Hebrews
1 and 2; Psalm 103:20

I. What angels are (Psalm 148:2, 5 KJV).

   A. Angels are individual beings created by God and either share in His plan for us (believers) or oppose His plan with Satan as their leader.

> Praise ye him, *all his angels:*
> praise ye him, all his hosts.
> Praise ye him, sun and moon:
> praise him, all ye stars of light.
> Praise him, ye heavens of heavens,
> and ye waters that be above the heavens.
> Let them praise the name of the Lord:
> for he commanded, *and they were created.*
> He hath also stablished them for ever and ever:
> He hath made a decree which shall not pass.

   B. Angel means messenger.

      1. Holy angels = *messengers of God*

> For whoever is ashamed of Me and My words in this adulterous and sinful generation, of

him the Son of Man also will be ashamed when He comes in the glory of His Father with the holy angels. (Mark 8:38 NKJ)

2. And they said, "Cornelius the centurion, a just man, one who fears God and has a good reputation among all the nation of the Jews, *was divinely instructed by a holy angel* to summon you to his house, and to hear words from you." (Acts 10:22 NKJ)

3. Fallen angels = messengers of Satan

C. Angels are mentioned in Old Testament 108 times and in the New Testament 165 times.
D. The work of angels is mentioned 300 times.
E. Angels are mentioned in 34 books of the Bible.
F. Angels are ministering spirits sent forth in the earth to minister to the heirs of salvation. (We should give a more earnest heed to this fact).
G. God created and designed angels for a specific purpose and ministry.
H. The Greek and Hebrew word for angel is "messenger" or "sent one."
I. We are called to walk in the supernatural and angels are here to help us.

Are they not all ministering spirits sent forth to minister for those who will inherit salvation? (Hebrews 1:14 NKJ)

Therefore we must give the more earnest heed to the things we have heard, lest we drift away. (Hebrews 2:1 NKJ)

For this reason [that is, because of God's final revelation in His Son Jesus and because of Jesus' superiority to the angels] *we must pay much closer attention than ever to the things that we have heard,* so that we do not [in any way] drift away from truth. For if the message given through angels [the Law given to Moses] was authentic and unalterable, and every violation and disobedient act received an appropriate penalty, how will we escape [the penalty] if we ignore such a great salvation [the gospel, the new covenant]? (Hebrews 2:1–3a AMP)

Angels are assigned to ministers and ministries.

I charge you before God and the Lord Jesus Christ and the elect angels that you observe these things without prejudice, doing nothing with partiality. Do not lay hands on anyone hastily, nor share in other people's sins; keep yourself pure. (1 Timothy 5:21–22 NKJ)

II. *What are angels capable of doing?*

And of the angels He says: *"Who makes His angels spirits And His ministers a flame of fire."* But to the Son He says: "Your throne, O God, is forever and ever.

A. Angels have superhuman strength.

Bless the Lord, you His angels, *who excel in strength,* who do His word, Heeding the voice of His word. Bless the Lord, all you His hosts, you minister of His, who do His pleasure. Bless the Lord, all His works, in all places of His dominion. (Psalm 103:20–22 NKJ)

Now after the Sabbath, as the first day of the week began to dawn, Mary Magdalene and the other Mary came to see the tomb. And behold, there was a great earthquake; *for an angel of the Lord descended from heaven and came and rolled back the stone from the door and sat on it.* His countenance was like lightning, and his clothing as white as snow. And the guards shook for fear of him and became like dead men. But the angel answered and said to the women, "Do not be afraid, for I know that you seek Jesus who was crucified. He is not here; for He is risen, as He said. Come, see the place where the Lord lay. And go quickly and tell His disciples that He is risen from the dead, and indeed He is going before you into Galilee; there you will see Him. Behold, I have told you." So, they went out quickly from the tomb with fear and great joy and ran to bring His disciple's word. (Matthew 28:1–8 NKJ)

B. Angels can manifest, look, and act like humans.
C. Angels are not babies.
D. Angels are not female (neither male nor female).
E. Angels are created by God.
F. Angels hearken to God's Word.
G. Angels are normally large.
H. Angels seek to understand redemption because it is a mystery to them.
I. Angels are not to be worshipped.
J. Angels are not to do for us the things we can do for ourselves.
K. Angels are here to help us do the things we can't do on our own.
L. We are not to seek angels, ask to see them, or ask to talk to them. God will not send you an angel and make it visible just so you will know what an angel looks like.
M. We are to speak the Word of God and command or send them according to the Word.
N. Angels are always with us. They are assigned to us at birth, maybe even at conception
O. Angels have assignments; they have specific jobs to carry out.
P. Angels are not all alike.
Q. Angels are not your dead relatives.
R. Angels have charge over you.
S. Angels can feed you.
T. Angels can clothe you.
U. Angels can be visible or invisible.

He is the image of the invisible God, the firstborn over all creation. For by Him all things were created that are in heaven and that are on earth, visible and invisible, whether thrones or dominions or principalities or powers. All things were created through Him and for Him. (Colossians 1:15–16 NKJ)

Yes, angels are on assignment to minister for you. They have been given a plan and a purpose just as you and I have a plan and purpose.

Example of angels on assignment, visible and invisible.

Now the king of Aram (Syria) was making war against Israel, and he consulted with his servants, saying, "My camp shall be in such and such a place." The man of God sent word to the king of Israel saying, "Be careful not to pass by this place, because the Arameans are pulling back to there." Then the king of Israel sent word to the place about which Elisha had warned him; so, he guarded himself there repeatedly.

Now the heart of the king of Aram (Syria) was enraged over this thing. He called his servants and said to them, "Will you not tell me which of us is helping the king of Israel?" One of his servants said, "None [of us is helping him], my lord, O king; but Elisha, the prophet who is in Israel, tells the king of Israel the words that you speak in your bedroom." So, he said, "Go and see where he is, so that I may send [men] and seize him." And he was told, "He is in Dothan." So, he sent horses and chariots and a powerful army there. They came by night and surrounded the city.

The servant of the man of God got up early and went out, and behold, there was an army with horses and chariots encircling the city. Elisha's servant said to him, "Oh no, my master! What are we to do?" Elisha answered, "Do not be afraid, for those who are with us are more than those who are with them." Then Elisha prayed and said,

> "Lord, please, open his eyes that he may see." *And the Lord opened the servants' eyes and he saw; and behold, the mountain was full of horses and chariots of fire surrounding Elisha.* (2 Kings 6:8–17 AMP)

Elisha was making a specific point when he said, "They that be with us are more than they that be with them." This was a faith statement.

Angels can be all around us even when we don't know they are. Be careful what you say and how you act. When we speak doubt and unbelief, we hinder the work of angels.

Hebrews 1:14 declares that angels are servants sent to care for us. The *Life Application Study Bible and New American Standard Bible,* has the following to say about Hebrews 1:14:

> Angels are God's messengers, spiritual beings created by God and under His authority (*Colossians 1:16*). They have several functions: serving believers (*Hebrews 1:14*), protecting the children (*Matthew 18:10*), proclaiming God's messages (*Revelation 14:6–12*), and executing God's judgment (*Acts 12:1–23; Revelation 20:1–3*).

It is our job to preach the gospel until the church is raptured, and then angels will take over and begin to preach the gospel to those who remain.

Spiritual Beings Created by God

> For by Him all things were created that are in heaven and that are on earth, visible and invisible, whether thrones or dominions or principalities or powers. All things were created through Him and for Him. (Colossians 1:16 NKJ)

Angels Serve Believers

> Are they not all ministering spirits sent forth to minister for those who will inherit salvation? (Hebrews 1:14 NKJ)

Angels Protect the Children

Take heed that you do not despise one of these little ones, for I say to you that in heaven their angels always see the face of My Father who is in heaven. For the Son of Man has come to save that which was lost. (Matthew 18:10–11 NKJ)

Angels Proclaim God's Messages

Then I saw another angel flying in the midst of heaven, having the everlasting gospel to preach to those who dwell on the earth—to every nation, tribe, tongue, and people—saying with a loud voice, "Fear God and give glory to Him, for the hour of His judgment has come; and worship Him who made heaven and earth, the sea and springs of water."

And another angel followed, saying, "Babylon is fallen, is fallen, that great city, because she has made all nations drink of the wine of the wrath of her fornication."

Then a third angel followed them, saying with a loud voice, "If anyone worships the beast and his image, and receives his mark on his forehead or on his hand, he himself shall also drink of the wine of the wrath of God, which is poured out full strength into the cup of His indignation. He shall be tormented with fire and brimstone in the presence of the holy angels and in the presence of the Lamb. And the smoke of their torment ascends forever and ever; and they have no rest day or night, who worship the beast and his image, and whoever receives the mark of his name."

Here is the patience of the saints; here are those who keep the commandments of God and the faith of Jesus. (Revelation 14:6–12 NKJ)

Angels Execute God's Judgement

> Then I saw an angel coming down from heaven, having the key to the bottomless pit and a great chain in his hand. He laid hold of the dragon, that serpent of old, who is the Devil and Satan, and bound him for a thousand years; and he cast him into the bottomless pit, and shut him up, and set a seal on him. (Revelation 20:1–3 NKJ)

Angels operate under the authority of Jesus *(1 Peter 3:22)*, and one of their jobs is ministering to believers. Our responsibility is to make sure that we are doing the will of our Father and that we are putting His Word in our mouths. When we do this, *Psalm 103:20* promises that angels carry out God's commands and are obedient to His Word. They act as enforcers of the Word and will of God in our lives.

> Who has gone into heaven and is at the right hand of God, angels and authorities and powers having been made subject to Him. (1 Peter 3:22 NKJ)

III. Are they not all ministering spirits sent forth to minister for them who shall be heirs of salvation?

> Are not the angels all ministering spirits (servants) sent out in the service [of God for the assistance] of those who are to inherit salvation? (Hebrews 1:14 AMPC)

IV. Most of us heard about our guardian angel when we were just children. And in those days, it was a comforting thought. With monsters lurking behind the closet door and creepy things crawling beneath the bed, it was good to know that someone was there to protect us when the light was out.

But as the years passed, we outgrew our childhood fears. The imaginary creatures that had once seemed so real disappeared from our minds, and sadly enough, for most of us, the angels did too.

But angels are not just kid stuff. They're powerful spirits sent forth to minister for *us who are heirs of salvation.*

V. The word "salvation" in Hebrews 1:14 is from the Greek word *soteria*, meaning "deliverance, preservation—material and temporal deliverance." Just think about that! God has created vast numbers of gloriously powerful spiritual beings for the express purpose of protecting us and delivering us from the evils of this world.

And remember, according to *Psalm 103:20*, the Word of God is what puts those angels in action. So when you're in trouble, don't cower and cry about how awful things are. Speak the Word! Give your angels something to respond to, then be patient and let them have time to work. They'll get their job done.

VI. Scripture reading:

> But the mercy and loving-kindness of the Lord are from everlasting to everlasting upon those who reverently and worshipfully fear Him, and His righteousness is to children's children— To such as keep His covenant [hearing, receiving, loving, and obeying it] and to those who [earnestly] remember His commandments to do them [imprinting them on their hearts]. The Lord has established His throne in the heavens, and His kingdom rules overall. *Bless (affectionately, gratefully praise) the Lord, you His angels, you mighty ones who do His commandments, hearkening to the voice of His word.* Bless (affectionately, gratefully praise) the Lord, all you His hosts, you His ministers who do His pleasure. Bless the Lord, all His works in all places of His dominion; bless (affectionately, gratefully praise) the Lord, O my soul! (Psalm 103:17–22 AMPC)

VII. Origin of angels

A. Created by God

1. Praise Him all His angels; Praise Him all His hosts. (Psalm 148:2)

2. For by him all things were created: things in heaven and on earth, visible and invisible, whether thrones or powers or rulers or authorities; all things were created by him and for him. (Colossians 1:16)

B. Created before man and earth

1. In the beginning God created heaven and earth. (Genesis 1:1)

2. Job 38:4–7: "sons of God" = angels

C. All angels were created holy.

1. Genesis 1:21: God created everything good. (He could not create everything good and create evil angels at the same time.)
2. Genesis gap theory: something happened between Genesis 1:1 and Genesis 1:2.

   a) Indefinite time gap between Genesis 1:1 and Genesis 1:2
   b) Genesis 1:1: God created the world perfect.

      (1) A perfect world would not be void and without form.
      (2) Lucifer was the ruling angel over earth before Adam was created.
      (3) Lucifer rebelled against God (Isaiah 14) because of pride and was thrown out of heaven.
      (4) One-third of the angels followed him and were thrown out of heaven with him.
      (5) They came to earth and destroyed it.
      (6) These fallen angels became the evil angels of today.

3. Angels had a will and the ability to make choices then, which they do not have now.

VIII. General information about angels

God's invisible hosts are better organized than any of the armies of man—or Satan.

Angels think, feel, and display emotions. They have a will but not free will. Evidently, when they were created, they had free will to choose.

Angel's guide, comfort, and provide for people during suffering and persecution.

At death, the faithful will be ushered by angels into the presence of God.

A. They are spirit.

1. Psalm 104:1, 4

   Bless the Lord, O my soul.
   Who makes His angels spirits.

2. Are they not all ministering spirits, sent forth to minister for them who shall be heirs of salvation? (Hebrews 1:14)

3. They do not have bodies the same as we do. (Jesus said "A spirit does not have flesh and bone as you see me have.")

   But they were terrified and frightened, and supposed they had seen a spirit. And He said to them, "Why are you troubled? And why do doubts arise in your hearts? Behold My hands and My feet, that it is I Myself. Handle Me and see, for a spirit does not have flesh and bones as you see I have." (Luke 24:37–39)

4. They stand in a freer relation to time and space than we do.

   a) Many can be in a small place at the same time.
   b) *Luke 8:30* relates the story of a demon-possessed man. Jesus asked the spirit in the man what his name was. He answered, "Legion, because there

are many of us." Legion was largest unit in Roman army, between three thousand to six thousand.

5. They are not omnipresent. They can only be in one place at a time.
6. They are not to be worshipped (Romans 1:25; Colossians 2:18; Revelation 19:10 NKJ)

Therefore, God also gave them up to uncleanness, in the lusts of their hearts, to dishonor their bodies among themselves, who exchanged the truth of God for the lie, and worshiped and served the creature rather than the Creator, who is blessed forever. Amen. (Romans 1:24)

Beware lest anyone cheat you through philosophy and empty deceit, according to the tradition of men, according to the basic principles of the world, and not according to Christ. (Colossians 2:18)

Then he said to me, "Write: Blessed are those who are called to the marriage supper of the Lamb!" And he said to me, "These are the true sayings of God." And I fell at his feet to worship him. But he said to me, "See that you do not do that! I am your fellow servant, and of your brethren who have the testimony of Jesus. Worship God! For the testimony of Jesus is the spirit of prophecy." (Revelation 19:10)

Let no man beguile you of your reward in a voluntary humility and worshipping of angels, intruding into those things which he hath not seen, vainly puffed up by his fleshly mind. (Colossians 2:18)

And I fell at his feet to worship him. And he said unto me, see thou do it not: I am thy fellow servant, and of thy brethren that have the testimony of Jesus: worship God: for the testimony of Jesus is the spirit of prophecy. (Revelation 19:10)

7. On many occasions, angels assumed the form of human bodies.

Now the two angels came to Sodom in the evening, and Lot was sitting in the gate of Sodom. When Lot saw them, he rose to meet them, and he bowed himself with his face toward the ground. And he said, "Here now, my lords, please turn in to your servant's house and spend the night and wash your feet; then you may rise early and go on your way." (Genesis 19:1)

Now in the sixth month the angel Gabriel was sent by God to a city of Galilee named Nazareth, to a virgin betrothed to a man whose name was Joseph, of the house of David. The virgin's name was Mary. And having come in, the angel said to her, "Rejoice, highly favored one, the Lord is with you; blessed are you among women!" (Luke 1:26–27)

And she saw two angels in white sitting, one at the head and the other at the feet, where the body of Jesus had lain. Then they said to her, "Woman, why are you weeping?" (John 20:12)

Now an angel of the Lord spoke to Philip, saying, "Arise and go toward the south along the road which goes down from Jerusalem to Gaza." This is desert. (Acts 8:26)

Now behold, an angel of the Lord stood by him, and a light shone in the prison; and he struck Peter on the side and raised him up, saying, "Arise quickly!" And his chains fell off his hands. Then the angel said to him, "Gird yourself and tie on your sandals"; and so, he did. And he said to him, "Put on your garment and follow me." (Acts 12:7–8)

Do not forget to entertain strangers, for by so doing some have unwittingly entertained angels. (Hebrews 13:2)

8.   They are a company, not a race.

   a)   All were created at one time.
   b)   They do not marry, reproduce, or die.

According to scripture in the Old Testament there was a time when fallen angels took human females as their wives. They had sexual relations with them, and many scholars believe this is where the giants came from, that is discussed in the Old Testament. This is found in Genesis the 6th chapter.

Jesus answered and said to them, "The sons of this age marry and are given in marriage. But those who are counted worthy to attain that age, and the resurrection from the dead, neither marry nor are given in marriage; nor can they die anymore, for they are equal to the angels and are sons of God, being sons of the resurrection. But even Moses showed in the burning bush passage that the dead are raised, when he called the Lord the God of Abraham, the God of Isaac, and the God of Jacob.' For He is not the God of the dead but of the living, for all live to Him." (Luke 20:34–36)

   c)   Angels are created beings and were all created at the same time.

B.   Number of angels

   1.   Revelations 5:11: 10,000 x 10,000 + thousands of thousands = hundreds of millions of angels and around the throne of God
   2.   Hebrews 12:22: *innumerable*
   3.   Job 25:3: One translation says, "Who are able to number the angels?"

C. Nature of angels

Have intelligence

1. Angels desire to investigate our salvation.

To them it was revealed that, not to themselves, but to us they were ministering the things which now have been reported to you through those who have preached the gospel to you by the Holy Spirit sent from heaven—things which angels desire to look into. (1 Peter 1:12)

2. Angels communicate intelligently in speech. They have their own language.

Though I speak with the tongues of men and of angels, but have not love, I have become sounding brass or a clanging cymbal. (1 Corinthians 13:1)

3. They can communicate in any language, and they communicate with each other in their own language.

Then the Angel of the Lord admonished Joshua, saying, "Thus says the Lord of hosts: 'If you will walk in My ways, and if you will keep My command, then you shall also judge My house, And likewise have charge of My courts; I will give you places to walk Among these who stand here. (Zechariah 3:6–7)

Above it stood seraphim; each one had six wings: with two he covered his face, with two he covered his feet, and with two he flew. And one cried to another and said: "Holy, holy, holy is the Lord of hosts; The whole earth is full of His glory!" (Isaiah 6:2–3)

4.   They can talk to men.

Then an angel of the Lord appeared to him, standing on the right side of the altar of incense. And when Zacharias saw him, he was troubled, and fear fell upon him. But the angel said to him, "Do not be afraid, Zacharias, for your prayer is heard; and your wife Elizabeth will bear you a son, and you shall call his name John. And you will have joy and gladness, and many will rejoice at his birth. For he will be great in the sight of the Lord and shall drink neither wine nor strong drink. He will also be filled with the Holy Spirit, even from his mother's womb. And he will turn many of the children of Israel to the Lord their God. He will also go before Him in the spirit and power of Elijah, 'to turn the hearts of the fathers to the children,' and the disobedient to the wisdom of the just, to make ready a people prepared for the Lord." And Zacharias said to the angel, "How shall I know this? For I am an old man, and my wife is well advanced in years." And the angel answered and said to him, "I am Gabriel, who stands in the presence of God, and was sent to speak to you and bring you these glad tidings. But behold, you will be mute and not able to speak until the day these things take place, because you did not believe my words which will be fulfilled in their own time." And the people waited for Zacharias, and marveled that he lingered so long in the temple. But when he came out, he could not speak to them; and they perceived that he had seen a vision in the temple, for he beckoned to them and remained speechless. So it was, as soon as the days of his service were completed, that he departed to his own house. Now after those days his wife Elizabeth conceived; and she hid herself five months, saying, "Thus the Lord has dealt with me, in the days when He looked on me, to take away my reproach among people." (Luke 1:11–23)

Now an angel of the Lord spoke to Philip, saying, "Arise and go toward the south along the road which goes down from Jerusalem to Gaza." This is desert. (Acts 8:26)

5. Angels have names.

Having become so much better than the angels, as He has by inheritance obtained a more excellent name than they. (Hebrews 1:4)

Angels have wisdom and knowledge beyond man about many things.

To bring about this change of affairs your servant Joab has done this thing; but my lord is wise, according to the wisdom of the angel of God, to know everything that is in the earth." (2 Samuel 14:20)

6. They are not all-knowing but growing in knowledge.

And to make all see what is the fellowship of the mystery, which from the beginning of the ages has been hidden in God who created all things through Jesus Christ; to the intent that now the manifold wisdom of God might be made known by the church to the principalities and powers in the heavenly places. (Ephesians 3:9–10)

To them it was revealed that, not to themselves, but to us they were ministering the things which now have been reported to you through those who have preached the gospel to you by the Holy Spirit sent from heaven—things which angels desire to look into. (1 Peter 1:12)

7. Angels can speak but not appear. This is normally how they will communicate with humans. They may speak

to you and warn you of coming danger or advise you in a situation.

Now an angel of the Lord spoke to Philip, saying, "Arise and go toward the south along the road which goes down from Jerusalem to Gaza." This is desert. (Acts 8:26)

8. The Holy Spirit speaks to us from within, but angels speak from the outside and your spirit man picks it up. That's why you may think you heard a voice and when you look around no one is there and no one else heard what you heard.

D. Angels have emotions.

1. They rejoice over a sinner saved.

Likewise, I say to you, there is joy in the presence of the angels of God over one sinner who repents. (Luke 15:10)

2. They rejoiced over birth of Jesus with great exuberance (*Luke 2*).
3. Most are large—some nine feet tall with no wings.
4. Cherubim, seraphim, created beings who have wings
5. Appearance of angels

Bless the Lord, you His angels, who excel in strength, who do His word, Heeding the voice of His word. Bless the Lord, all you His hosts, you minister of His, who do His pleasure. (Psalm 103:20–21)

Are they not all ministering spirits sent forth to minister for those who will inherit salvation? (Hebrews 1:14)

6. Angels had a will to choose at one time but not now. Before they rebelled and were cast out of heaven, they

had the free will to choose. We believe they had a free will until the time of Noah's flood that destroyed the earth. From this point on they had a will but not free will. You might say God had to reprogram the angels after Noah's flood to keep them from trying to take females as their wives and from rebelling.

7.   Angels experience joy.

Likewise, I say to you, there is joy in the presence of the angels of God over one sinner who repents. (Luke 15:10)

E.   Their bodies are not discussed in the Bible.

1.   They will appear as oriental to Orientals, Russian to Russians, African to Africans, American to Americans—every nationality and race of world.

Do not forget to entertain strangers, for by so doing some have unwittingly entertained angels. (Hebrews 13:2)

F.   They move through space swiftly.

Yes, while I was speaking in prayer, the man Gabriel, whom I had seen in the vision at the beginning, being caused to fly swiftly, reached me about the time of the evening offering. (Daniel 9:21)

G.   We are not usually aware of their presence. They do not make visible appearances most of the time but can if their presence is necessary to carry out an assignment.

H.   Angels mainly appear in masculine form and on one occasion in the Bible, they appeared as female. The Bible says they were not created male or female, but they can take on the form of either one.

Then I raised my eyes and looked, and there were two women, coming with the wind in their wings; for they had wings like the wings of a stork, and they lifted up the basket between earth and heaven. (Zechariah 5:9)

I.   Their appearance is awesome.

Now after the Sabbath, as the first day of the week began to dawn, Mary Magdalene and the other Mary came to see the tomb. And behold, there was a great earthquake; for an angel of the Lord descended from heaven and came and rolled back the stone from the door and sat on it. His countenance was like lightning, and his clothing as white as snow. And the guards shook for fear of him and became like dead men. But the angel answered and said to the women, "Do not be afraid, for I know that you seek Jesus who was crucified." (Matthew 28:1–5)

J.   Angels are mighty in strength.

Bless the Lord, you His angels,
Who excel in strength, who do His word,
Heeding the voice of His word. (Psalm 103:20)

K.   They can appear as human beings and as strangers. Angels are not male or female but can manifest as needed in human form.

Do not forget to entertain strangers, for by so doing some have unwittingly entertained angels. (Hebrews 13:2)

L.   Angels can be visible or invisible.

M.   Angels have names.

Having become so much better than the angels, as He has by inheritance obtained a more excellent name than they. (Hebrews 1:4)

N.   Angels have great power and authority.

O.   Angels have greater power than man.

Whereas angels, who are greater in power and might, do not bring a reviling accusation against them before the Lord. (2 Peter 2:11)

P.   Not all-powerful as God but have great strength.

Bless the Lord, you His angels, who excel in strength, who do His word, Heeding the voice of His word. (Psalm 103:20)

1.   They rolled back the stone that could have weighed two tons.

Now after the Sabbath, as the first day of the week began to dawn, Mary Magdalene and the other Mary came to see the tomb. And behold, there was a great earthquake; for an angel of the Lord descended from heaven and came and rolled back the stone from the door and sat on it. (Matthew 28:1–2)

2.   They closed the mouths of lions.

My God sent His angel and shut the lions' mouths, so that they have not hurt me, because I was found innocent before Him; and also, O king, I have done no wrong before you. (Daniel 6:22)

3.   They opened prison doors and loosed chains.

Peter was therefore kept in prison, but constant prayer was offered to God for him by the church. And when Herod was about to bring him out, that night Peter was sleeping, bound with two chains between two soldiers; and the guards before the door were keeping the prison. Now behold, an angel of the Lord stood by him, and a light shone in the prison; and he struck Peter on the side and raised him up, saying, "Arise quickly!" And his chains fell off his hands. Then the angel said to him, "Gird yourself and tie on your sandals"; and so, he did. And he said to him, "Put on your garment and follow me." So, he went out and followed him, and did not know that what was done by the angel was real, but thought he was seeing a vision. When they were past the first and the second guard posts, they came to the iron gate that leads to the city, which opened to them of its own accord; and they went out and went down one street, and immediately the angel departed from him. And when Peter had come to himself, he said, "Now I know for certain that the Lord has sent His angel and has delivered me from the hand of Herod and from all the expectation of the Jewish people." So, when he had considered this, he came to the house of Mary, the mother of John whose surname was Mark, where many were gathered together praying. And as Peter knocked at the door of the gate, a girl named Rhoda came to answer. When she recognized Peter's voice, because of her gladness she did not open the gate, but ran in and announced that Peter stood before the gate. But they said to her, "You are beside yourself!" Yet she kept insisting that it was so. So, they said, "It is his angel." (Acts 12:5–10)

4.   They can provide protection.

For He shall give His angels charge over you, to keep you in all your ways. (Psalm 91:11)

The angel of the Lord encamps all around those who fear Him And delivers them. (Psalm 34:7)

Let those be put to shame and brought to dishonor Who seek after my life; Let those be turned back and brought to confusion Who plot my hurt. Let them be like chaff before the wind and let the angel of the Lord chase them. Let their way be dark and slippery, and let the angel of the Lord pursue them. For without cause they have hidden their net for me in a pit, which they have dug without cause for my life. Let destruction come upon him unexpectedly and let his net that he has hidden catch himself; Into that very destruction let him fall. (Psalm 35:4–8)

5. Angels can help us, warn us. They can defend us and protect us.
6. In the Hebrew language, the word *delivereth* means to "escape wholly and to deliver wholly."
7. *Exodus 23:20–23* says that angels can defend you, and in *Psalm 35:1–4*, it says that He will be an enemy to my enemies.

Behold, I send an Angel before you to keep you in the way and to bring you into the place which I have prepared. Beware of Him and obey His voice; do not provoke Him, for He will not pardon your transgressions; for My name is in Him. But if you indeed obey His voice and do all that I speak, then I will be an enemy to your enemies and an adversary to your adversaries. For My Angel will go before you and bring you in to the Amorites and the Hittites and the Perizzites and the Canaanites and the Hivites and the Jebusites; and I will cut them off. You shall not bow down to their gods, nor serve them, nor do according to their works; but you shall utterly overthrow them and completely break down their sacred pillars. (Exodus 23:20–23)

You can provoke angels by not doing what they tell you to do or by speaking doubt and unbelief in their presence.

Plead my cause, O Lord, with those who strive with me; Fight against those who fight against me. Take hold of shield and buckler and stand up for my help. Also draw out the spear,

And stop those who pursue me. Say to my soul, "I am your salvation." Let those be put to shame and brought to dishonor

Who seek after my life; Let those be turned back and brought to confusion Who plot my hurt. (Psalm 35:1–5)

8. The angels began to defend and surround us to protect us as we reverence God and speak His Word.
9. We see in *Psalm 35* that all we must do is stand and "let them be as a chaff before the wind and to let the angel chase them" and their "way will be dark and slippery."
10. Angels bring deliverance for us in difficult times and situations.
11. A Roman legion was 6,000 soldiers. Jesus said if He asked, His Father would send 12 legions of angels. That's 72,000 mighty, heavenly angels.

But Jesus said to him, "Put your sword in its place, for all who take the sword will perish by the sword. Or do you think that I cannot now pray to My Father, and He will provide Me with more than twelve legions of angels?" (Matthew 26:52–53)

12. Second Kings 19:35 says one angel killed 185,000 of Assyrian's finest fighting soldiers.

And it came to pass on a certain night that the angel of the Lord went out and killed in the camp of the Assyrians one hundred and eighty-five thousand; and when people arose early in the morning, there were the corpses—all dead.

The Message translation reads, "And it so happened that that very night an angel of God came and massacred a hundred and eighty-five thousand Assyrians. When the people of Jerusalem got up next morning, there it was—a whole camp of corpses!"

CHAPTER 2

Angels, Man, and Jesus

I.   Angels and their relationship to man and Jesus

    A.   Angels want to understand redemption.

        To them it was revealed that, not to themselves, but to us they were ministering the things which now have been reported to you through those who have preached the gospel to you by the Holy Spirit sent from heaven—things which angels desire to look into. (1 Peter 1:12)

        The prophets who told us this was coming asked a lot of questions about this gift of life God was preparing. The Messiah's Spirit let them in on some of it—that the Messiah would experience suffering, followed by glory. They clamored to know who and when. All they were told was that they were serving you, you who by orders from heaven have now heard for yourselves—through the Holy Spirit—the Message of those prophecies fulfilled. Do you realize how fortunate you are? Angels would have given anything to be in on this! (1 Peter 1:10–12 MSG)

B.   Angels observe believers' affairs.

> For I think that God has displayed us, the apostles, last, as men condemned to death; for we have been made a spectacle to the world, both to angels and to men. (1 Corinthians 4:9)

> For man is not from woman, but woman from man. Nor was man created for the woman, but woman for the man. For this reason, the woman ought to have a symbol of authority on her head, because of the angels. (1 Corinthians 11:8–10)

> I charge you before God and the Lord Jesus Christ and the elect angels that you observe these things without prejudice, doing nothing with partiality. (1 Timothy 5:21)

C.   Angels want to gain better understanding of God's wisdom as it is displayed through the church.

> And to make all see what is the fellowship of the mystery, which from the beginning of the ages has been hidden in God who created all things through Jesus Christ; to the intent that now the manifold wisdom of God might be made known by the church to the principalities and powers in the heavenly places. (Ephesians 3:9–10)

D.   Angels minister to us in numerous ways.

1.   Find things for us
2.   Bring witnesses to witness to people we ask them to
3.   Protect us
4.   Minister on our behalf
5.   Comfort us and give direction
6.   They can defend you.

> Behold, I send an Angel before you to keep you in the way and to bring you into the place

which I have prepared. Beware of Him and obey His voice; do not provoke Him, for He will not pardon your transgressions; for My name is in Him. But if you indeed obey His voice and do all that I speak, then I will be an enemy to your enemies and an adversary to your adversaries. For My Angel will go before you and bring you in to the Amorites and the Hittites and the Perizzites and the Canaanites and the Hivites and the Jebusites; and I will cut them off. (Exodus 23:20–23)

Plead my cause, O Lord, with those who strive with me; Fight against those who fight against me. Take hold of shield and buckler and stand up for my help. Also draw out the spear and stop those who pursue me. Say to my soul, "I am your salvation." Let those be put to shame and brought to dishonor

Who seek after my life; Let those be turned back and brought to confusion Who plot my hurt. Let them be like chaff before the wind and let the angel of the Lord chase them. Let their way be dark and slippery, and let the angel of the Lord pursue them. (Psalm 35:1–5)

7.   Angels help during times of temptation.

For if God did not spare the angels who sinned, but cast them down to hell and delivered them into chains of darkness, to be reserved for judgment; and did not spare the ancient world, but saved Noah, one of eight people, a preacher of righteousness, bringing in the flood on the world of the ungodly; and turning the cities of Sodom and Gomorrah into ashes, condemned them to destruction, making them an example to those who afterward would live ungodly; and delivered righteous Lot, who was oppressed by the filthy conduct of the wicked (for that righteous man, dwelling among them, tormented his righteous soul from day to day by seeing and hearing their lawless deeds)—then the Lord knows how to deliver the godly out of temptations and to reserve the unjust under punishment for the day of judgment. (2 Peter 2:4–9)

Immediately the Spirit drove Him into the wilderness. And He was there in the wilderness forty days, tempted by Satan, and was with the wild beasts; and the angels ministered to Him. (Mark 1:12–13)

Now the two angels came to Sodom in the evening, and Lot was sitting in the gate of Sodom. When Lot saw them, he rose to meet them, and he bowed himself with his face toward the ground. And he said, "Here now, my lords, please turn in to your servant's house and spend the night and wash your feet; then you may rise early and go on your way." And they said, "No, but we will spend the night in the open square." But he insisted strongly; so, they turned in to him and entered his house. Then he made them a feast, and baked unleavened bread, and they ate.
Now before they lay down, the men of the city, the men of Sodom, both old and young, all the people from every quarter, surrounded the house. And they called to Lot and said to him, "Where are the men who came to you tonight? Bring them out to us that we may know them carnally." So, Lot went out to them through the doorway, shut the door behind him, and said, "Please, my brethren, do not do so wickedly! See now, I have two daughters who have not known a man; please, let me bring them out to you, and you may do to them as you wish; only do nothing to these men, since this is the reason, they have come under the shadow of my roof." And they said, "Stand back!" Then they said, "This one came in to stay here, and he keeps acting as a judge; now we will deal worse with you

than with them." So, they pressed hard against the man Lot, and came near to break down the door. But the men reached out their hands and pulled Lot into the house with them and shut the door. And they struck the men who were at the doorway of the house with blindness, both small and great, so that they became weary trying to find the door. Then the men said to Lot, "Have you anyone else here? Son-in-law, your sons, your daughters, and whomever you have in the city—take them out of this place! For we will destroy this place, because the outcry against them has grown great before the face of the Lord, and the Lord has sent us to destroy it." So, Lot went out and spoke to his sons-in-law, who had married his daughters, and said, "Get up, get out of this place; for the Lord will destroy this city!" But to his sons-in-law he seemed to be joking. *When the morning dawned, the angels urged Lot to hurry, saying, "Arise, take your wife and your two daughters who are here, lest you be consumed in the punishment of the city."* And while he lingered, the men took hold of his hand, his wife's hand, and the hands of his two daughters, the Lord being merciful to him, and they brought him out and set him outside the city. So it came to pass, when they had brought them outside, that he said, "Escape for your life! Do not look behind you nor stay anywhere in the plain. Escape to the mountains, lest you be destroyed." Then Lot said to them, "Please, no, my lords! Indeed now, your servant has found favor in your sight, and you have increased your mercy which you have shown me by saving my life; but I cannot escape to the mountains, lest some evil overtake me, and I die. (Genesis 19:1–19)

Then again, the one having the likeness of a man *touched me and strengthened me.* And he said, "O man greatly beloved, fear not! Peace be to you; be strong, yes, be strong!"

So when he spoke to me, I was strengthened, and said, "Let my lord speak, for you have
strengthened me." (*Daniel 10:18–19*)

8. Angels reveal things to us.

There was a certain man in Caesarea called
Cornelius, a centurion of what was called the
Italian Regiment, a devout man and one who
feared God with all his household, who gave alms
generously to the people, and prayed to God
always. About the ninth hour of the day, he saw
clearly in a vision an angel of God coming in and
saying to him, "Cornelius!"
And when he observed him, he was afraid,
and said, "What is it, lord?"
So he said to him, "Your prayers and your
alms have come up for a memorial before God.
Now send men to Joppa and send for Simon
whose surname is Peter. He is lodging with
Simon, a tanner, whose house is by the sea. He
will tell you what you must do." (Acts 10:1–6)

Then Joseph her husband, being a just man,
and not wanting to make her a public example,
was minded to put her away secretly. But while
he thought about these things, behold, an angel
of the Lord appeared to him in a dream, saying,
"Joseph, son of David, do not be afraid to take to
you Mary your wife, for that which is conceived
in her is of the Holy Spirit. (Matthew 1:19–20)

Now when they had departed, behold, an
angel of the Lord appeared to Joseph in a dream,
saying, "Arise, take the young Child and His
mother, flee to Egypt, and stay there until I bring
you word; for Herod will seek the young Child to
destroy Him." (Matthew 2:13)

Now when Herod was dead, behold, an angel of the Lord appeared in a dream to Joseph in Egypt, saying, "Arise, take the young Child and His mother, and go to the land of Israel, for those who sought the young Child's life are dead." (Matthew 2:19–20)

9.   Angels can bring food.

And Ahab told Jezebel all that Elijah had done, also how he had executed all the prophets with the sword. Then Jezebel sent a messenger to Elijah, saying, "So let the gods do to me, and more also, if I do not make your life as the life of one of them by tomorrow about this time." And when he saw that, he arose and ran for his life, and went to Beersheba, which belongs to Judah, and left his servant there.

But he himself went a day's journey into the wilderness and came and sat down under a broom tree. And he prayed that he might die, and said, "It is enough! Now, Lord, take my life, for I am no better than my fathers!"

Then as he lay and slept under a broom tree, *suddenly an angel touched him, and said to him, "Arise and eat." Then he looked, and there by his head was a cake baked on coals, and a jar of water. So, he ate and drank, and lay down again. And the angel of the Lord came back the second time, and touched him, and said, "Arise and eat, because the journey is too great for you." So, he arose, and ate and drank; and he went in the strength of that food forty days and forty nights as far as Horeb, the mountain of God.* (1 Kings 19:1–8)

10. In Daniel, we see that angels can lay hands on people.
11. Angels can help with prosperity.

Beloved, I pray that you may prosper in all things and be in health, just as your soul prospers. (3 John 1:2)

Bless the Lord, you His angels,
Who excel in strength, who do His word,
Heeding the voice of His word.
Bless the Lord, all you His hosts,
You ministers of His, who do His pleasure.
Bless the Lord, all His works,
In all places of His dominion.
Bless the Lord, O my soul! (Psalm 103: 20–21)

But you shall go to my father's house and to my family and take a wife for my son.' And I said to my master, 'Perhaps the woman will not follow me.' But he said to me, 'The Lord, before whom I walk, will send His angel with you and prosper your way; and you shall take a wife for my son from my family and from my father's house. (Genesis 24:38–40)

And he said to them, "Do not hinder me, since the Lord has prospered my way; send me away so that I may go to my master." (Genesis 24:56)

II. Jesus and angels (Hebrews 1:5–14)

A. Verse 4: Jesus is greater than angels, both in power and authority.
B. Verse 14: Jesus is our King and High Priest. Angels (ministering spirits) are sent on His behalf to minister to us and for us.
C. Jesus is eternal and so are the created angels.
D. Angels are holy.
E. Angels were created to serve Jesus.

For whoever is ashamed of Me and My words in this adulterous and sinful generation, of him the Son of Man also will be ashamed when He comes in the glory of His Father with the holy angels. (Mark 8:38)

And they said, "Cornelius the centurion, a just man, one who fears God and has a good reputation among all the nation of the Jews, was divinely instructed by a holy angel to summon you to his house, and to hear words from you." Then he invited them in and lodged them. (Acts 10:22)

F.   Angels can execute judgment for God.

Which is manifest evidence of the righteous judgment of God, that you may be counted worthy of the kingdom of God, for which you also suffer; since it is a righteous thing with God to repay with tribulation those who trouble you, and to give you who are troubled rest with us when the Lord Jesus is revealed from heaven with His mighty angels, in flaming fire taking vengeance on those who do not know God, and on those who do not obey the gospel of our Lord Jesus Christ. These shall be punished with everlasting destruction from the presence of the Lord and from the glory of His power. (2 Thessalonians 1:5–9)

III. Angel of the Lord

A.   Only found in the Old Testament as "an Angel of the Lord." In the New Testament, it is worded as "the Angel of the Lord." The term is found fifty-three times in the Old Testament and eleven times in the New Testament.
B.   After Jesus is born, we do not see the term "Angel of the Lord" again in scriptures.
C.   Jesus in the Old Testament is believed to be the "Angel of the Lord."

1.   Hagar fleeing from Abraham's house (verse 13: Hagar recognizes the angel as God)

Now the Angel of the Lord found her by a spring of water in the wilderness, by the spring on the way to Shur. And He said, "Hagar, Sarai's maid, where have you come from, and where are you going?"

She said, "I am fleeing from the presence of my mistress Sarai."

The Angel of the Lord said to her, "Return to your mistress, and submit yourself under her hand." Then the Angel of the Lord said to her, "I will multiply your descendants exceedingly, so that they shall not be counted for multitude." And the Angel of the Lord said to her: "Behold, you are with child,

And you shall bear a son. You shall call his name Ishmael, Because the Lord has heard your affliction. He shall be a wild man; His hand shall be against every man, And every man's hand against him. And he shall dwell in the presence of all his brethren."

Then she called the name of the Lord who spoke to her, You-Are-the-God-Who-Sees; for she said, "Have I also here seen Him who sees me?" Therefore, the well was called Beer Lahai Roi; observe, it is between Kadesh and Bered. (Genesis 16:7–14)

2.   Sacrifice of Isaac (verse 12: "From me" refers to God.)

Isaac did not see an angel but heard the angel's voice.

But the Angel of the Lord called to him from heaven and said, "Abraham, Abraham!"

So he said, "Here I am."

And He said, "Do not lay your hand on the lad, or do anything to him; for now I know that you fear God, since you have not withheld your son, your only son, from Me."

Then Abraham lifted his eyes and looked, and there behind him was a ram caught in a thicket by its horns. So, Abraham went and took the ram, and offered it up for a burnt offering instead of his son. And Abraham called the name of the place, The-Lord-Will-Provide; as it is said to this day, "In the Mount of the Lord it shall be provided."

Then the Angel of the Lord called to Abraham a second time out of heaven, and said: "By Myself I have sworn, says the Lord, because you have done this thing, and have not withheld your son, your only son—blessing I will bless you, and multiplying I will multiply your descendants as the stars of the heaven and as the sand which is on the seashore; and your descendants shall possess the gate of their enemies. In your seed all the nations of the earth shall be blessed, because you have obeyed My voice." So, Abraham returned to his young men, and they rose and went together to Beersheba; and Abraham dwelt at Beersheba. (Genesis 22:11–18)

3. Moses and the burning bush (verse: 4—referred to as God).

The angel appeared and spoke to Moses.

Now Moses was tending the flock of Jethro his father-in-law, the priest of Midian. And he led the flock to the back of the desert, and came to Horeb, the mountain of God. And the Angel of the Lord appeared to him in a flame of fire from the midst of a bush. So, he looked, and behold, the bush was burning with fire, but the bush was not consumed. Then Moses said, "I will now turn aside and see this great sight, why the bush does not burn." So, when the Lord saw that he turned aside to look, God called to him from the midst of the bush and said, "Moses, Moses!" And he said, "Here I am."

Then He said, "Do not draw near this place. Take your sandals off your feet, for the place where you stand is holy ground." (Exodus 3:1–5)

4.   Gideon (verse 14: "*Then the Lord turned to him*")

The angel appeared and spoke to Gideon.

Now the Angel of the Lord came and sat under the terebinth tree, which was in Ophrah, which belonged to Joash the Abiezrite, while his son Gideon threshed wheat in the winepress, in order to hide it from the Midianites. And the Angel of the Lord appeared to him, and said to him, "The Lord is with you, you mighty man of valor!"

Gideon said to Him, "O my lord, if the Lord is with us, why then has all this happened to us? And where are all His miracles which our fathers told us about, saying, 'Did not the Lord bring us up from Egypt?' But now the Lord has forsaken us and delivered us into the hands of the Midianites."

Then the Lord turned to him and said, "Go in this might of yours, and you shall save Israel from the hand of the Midianites. Have I not sent you?"

So he said to Him, "O my Lord, how can I save Israel? Indeed my clan is the weakest in Manasseh, and I am the least in my father's house."

And the Lord said to him, "Surely I will be with you, and you shall defeat the Midianites as one man."

Then he said to Him, "If now I have found favor in Your sight, then show me a sign that it is You who talk with me. Do not depart from here, I pray, until I come to You and bring out my offering and set it before You."

And He said, "I will wait until you come back."

So Gideon went in and prepared a young goat, and unleavened bread from an ephah of flour. The meat he put in a basket, and he put the broth in a pot; and he brought them out to Him under the terebinth tree and presented them. The Angel of God said to him, "Take the meat and the unleavened bread and lay them on this rock and pour out the broth." And he did so.

Then the Angel of the Lord put out the end of the staff that was in His hand and touched the meat and the unleavened bread; and fire rose out of the rock and consumed the meat and the unleavened bread. And the Angel of the Lord departed out of his sight.

Now Gideon perceived that He was the Angel of the Lord. So, Gideon said, "Alas, O Lord God! For I have seen the Angel of the Lord face to face."

Then the Lord said to him, "Peace be with you; do not fear, you shall not die." So, Gideon built an altar there to the Lord, and called it The-Lord-Is-Peace. To this day it is still in Ophrah of the Abiezrites. (Judges 6:11–23)

5. When Elijah fled from Jezebel.

The Angel appeared, he spoke and fed Elijah.

Then as he lay and slept under a broom tree, suddenly an angel touched him, and said to him, "Arise and eat." Then he looked, and there by his head was a cake baked on coals, and a jar of water. So, he ate and drank, and lay down again. And the angel of the LORD came back the second time, and touched him, and said, "Arise and eat, because the journey is too great for you." So, he arose and ate and drank; and he went in the strength of that food forty days and forty nights as far as Horeb, the mountain of God. (1 Kings 19:5–8)

6. One angel slew 185,000 Assyrian soldiers when surrounded in Jerusalem.

If one angel killed 185,000 soldiers, we can have assurance they can and will protect us also.

And it came to pass on a certain night that the angel of the Lord went out and killed in the camp of the Assyrians one hundred and eighty-five thousand; and when people arose early in the morning, there were the corpses—all dead. (2 Kings 19:35)

CHAPTER 3

Three Heavens

Where Do Angels Reside or Live?

I. Third heaven

> It is doubtless not profitable for me to boast. I will come to visions and revelations of the Lord: I know a man in Christ who fourteen years ago—whether in the body I do not know, or whether out of the body I do not know, God knows—such a one was caught up to the third heaven. (2 Corinthians 12:1–2)

A. If there is a third heaven, there must be two more.
B. "Highest heaven"

> Indeed heaven and the highest heavens belong to the Lord your God, also the earth with all that is in it. (Deuteronomy 10:14)

"Higher than the heavens" shows there are no more than three.

> For such a High Priest was fitting for us, who is holy, harmless, undefiled, separate from sinners, and has become higher than the heavens. (Hebrews 7:26)

C. Where God's throne is and where He is

> Do not be rash with your mouth,
> And let not your heart utter anything hastily
> before God.
> For God is in heaven, and you on earth;
> Therefore let your words be few. (Ecclesiastes 5:2)

D. Where many of the godly angels reside when not on assignment here on earth.

II. Stellar heaven or second heaven—stars and planets

A. And lest thou lift up thine eyes unto heaven, and when thou seest the sun, and the moon, and the stars, [even] all the host of heaven, shouldest be driven to worship them, and serve them, which the LORD thy God hath divided unto all nations under the whole heaven. (Deuteronomy 4:19)

B. And he put down the idolatrous priests, whom the kings of Judah had ordained to burn incense in the high places in the cities of Judah, and in the places round about Jerusalem; them also that burned incense unto Baal, to the sun, and to the moon, and to the planets, and to all the host of heaven. (2 Kings 23:5)

III. Atmospheric heaven or first heaven

A. This is where Satan, evil angels, and demon spirits live.

B. For our struggle is not against flesh and blood, but against the rulers, against the authorities, against the powers of this dark world and against the spiritual forces of evil in the heavenly realms. (Ephesians 6:12)

C. Paul warns against angels "from heaven" who would preach a false gospel.

> But even if we or an angel from heaven should
> preach a gospel other than the one, we preached to
> you, let him be eternally condemned! (Galatians 1:8)

D. At the time of Lucifer's rebellion, when one-third of the angels followed him, they fell from the third heaven and now abide in the atmospheric heaven.

E. Evil angels cannot be in the third heaven except Satan.

> Now there was a day when the sons of God came to present themselves before the Lord, and Satan also came among them. And the Lord said to Satan, "From where do you come?" So Satan answered the Lord and said, "From going to and fro on the earth, and from walking back and forth on it." (Job 1:6)

> Then I heard a loud voice saying in heaven, "Now salvation, and strength, and the kingdom of our God, and the power of His Christ have come, for the accuser of our brethren, who accused them before our God Day and night, has been cast down." (Revelations 12:10)

Note: In 2 Peter 2:4, it says angels were cast down into hell and chained to be held for judgment. The Bible is not clear, but it appears some fallen angels were chained, and some were loosed on the earth to serve as Satan directs them. We know that Satan, fallen or evil angels, and demons roam and rule the earth, causing deception, chaos, and confusion.

CHAPTER 4

Organization and Classification of Angels

I. General information

A. For God is not a God of disorder but of peace. God is a God of order and organization, not confusion. (1 Corinthians 14:33)

B. All angels were created good and holy, and God classified them when they were created.

C. When Satan fell and took one-third of the angels with him, he kept their same rank but perverted their functions. Satan thinks of nothing new, just perverts what God has already done. His number one plan is deception.

D. The Bible clearly indicates that the angelic realm includes holy beings called angels, archangels, cherubim, and seraphim. It also suggests that there is organizational hierarchy of angels and demons.

E. Here is the order that most scholars believe angels fall into from the greatest rank to the least rank archangel, angels, seraphim, cherubim, principalities, authorities, powers, thrones, might, and dominion.

He is the image of the invisible God, the firstborn over all creation. For by Him all things were created that are in heaven and that are on earth, visible and invisible, whether thrones or dominions or principalities or powers. All things were created through Him and for Him. And He is before all things, and in Him all things consist. And He is the head of the body, the church, who is the beginning, the firstborn from the dead, that in all things He may have the preeminence. (Colossians 1:15–18)

Yet in all these things we are more than conquerors through Him who loved us. For I am persuaded that neither death nor life, nor angels nor principalities nor powers, nor things present nor things to come, nor height nor depth, nor any other created thing, shall be able to separate us from the love of God which is in Christ Jesus our Lord. (Romans 8:37–39)

F. In 1 Thessalonians 4:16, Paul seemed to be talking about and suggesting to a hierarchy in which some angels have more authority than others.

For the Lord Himself will descend from heaven with a shout, with the voice of an archangel, and with the trumpet of God. And the dead in Christ will rise first.

G. Over the centuries, church tradition helped to develop this hierarchy of angels and is made up of ten diverse levels: angels, archangels, principalities and authorities, powers, virtues, dominions, thrones, cherubim, and seraphim.

H. This list was probably formed from the teachings of Paul and his writings. Below is a list of those scriptures.

Yet in all these things we are more than conquerors through Him who loved us. For I am persuaded that neither death nor life, nor angels nor principalities nor powers, nor things present nor things to come, nor height nor depth, nor any other created thing, shall be able to separate us from the love of God which is in Christ Jesus our Lord. (Romans 8:37–39)

And what is the exceeding greatness of His power toward us who believe, according to the working of His mighty power which He worked in Christ when He raised Him from the dead and seated Him at His right hand in the heavenly places, far above all principality and power and might and dominion, and every name that is named, not only in this age but also in that which is to come. (Ephesians 1:19–21)

To me, who am less than the least of all the saints, this grace was given, that I should preach among the Gentiles the unsearchable riches of Christ, and to make all see what is the fellowship of the mystery, which from the beginning of the ages has been hidden in God who created all things through Jesus Christ; to the intent that now the manifold wisdom of God might be made known by the church to the principalities and powers in the heavenly places. (Ephesians 3:8–10)

For by Him all things were created that are in heaven and that are on earth, visible and invisible, whether thrones or dominions or principalities or powers. All things were created through Him and for Him. (Colossians 1:16)

There are many different opinions and beliefs concerning angels, their rank, and the various levels and ranks. But I believe it is clear from the Bible that there are different types of angels and that angels have different roles and positions within God's kingdom. Just as in the body of Christ, it is true among angels!

There are diversities of gifts, but the same Spirit. There are differences of ministries, but the same Lord. And there are diversities of activities, but it is the same God who works all in all. (1 Corinthians 12:4–6)

II. Classification and rank

A. *Archangel—high rank, chief prince* (Daniel 10:13). Michael was referred to as a high ranking angel, and the chief prince in the book of Daniel.

1. Bible scholars agree that there were at least two archangels, but Michael is the only one mentioned by name in scriptures. The other possibility and angel that was believed to be an archangel was Gabriel. Some scholars believe Lucifer could have been, but scriptures do not back up this theory. Lucifer was classified as cherubim in scripture.

But the prince of the kingdom of Persia withstood me twenty-one days; and behold, Michael, one of the chief princes, came to help me, for I had been left alone there with the kings of Persia. (Daniel 10:13)

2. Daniel 10:13 references that there were other archangels, "one of the chief princes."
3. There are only two places in the Bible where the word archangel is mentioned and only one place that he is explicitly named.

For if we believe that Jesus died and rose again, even so God will bring with Him those who sleep in Jesus. For this we say to you by the word of the Lord, that we who are alive and remain until the coming of the Lord will by no means precede those who are asleep. For the Lord Himself will descend from heaven with a shout, with the voice of an archangel, and with the trumpet of God. And the dead in Christ will rise first. Then we who are alive and remain shall be caught up together with them in the clouds to meet the Lord in the air. And thus we shall always be with the Lord. (1 Thessalonians 4:14–17)

Yet Michael the archangel, in contending with the devil, when he disputed about the body of Moses, dared not bring against him a reviling accusation, but said, "The Lord rebuke you!" (Jude 1:9)

4. Michael—Highest ranking angel in most scholars' opinion and was specifically called an archangel.

a) He is known as prince of God's people.
b) Michael appears in the Old and New Testament.

But the prince of the kingdom of Persia withstood me twenty-one days; and behold, Michael, one of the chief princes, came to help me, for I had been left alone there with the kings of Persia. (Daniel 10:13)

Then he said, "Do you know why I have come to you? And now I must return to fight with the prince of Persia; and when I have gone forth, indeed the prince of Greece will come. But I will tell you what is noted in the Scripture of Truth. (No one upholds me against these, except Michael your prince.) (Daniel 10:20–21)

At that time Michael shall stand up, The great prince who stands watch over the sons of your people; And there shall be a time of trouble, Such as never was since there was a nation, Even to that time. And at that time your people shall be delivered, Everyone who is found written in the book. (Daniel 12:1)

Yet Michael the archangel, in contending with the devil, when he disputed about the body of Moses, dared not bring against him a reviling accusation, but said, "The Lord rebuke you!" (Jude 9)

c)   Michael means "who is like God?"
d)   Michael has warring capabilities (Daniel 10).

And war broke out in heaven: Michael and his angels fought with the dragon; and the dragon and his angels fought, but they did not prevail, nor was a place found for them in heaven any longer. So, the great dragon was cast out, that serpent of old, called the Devil and Satan, who deceives the whole world; he was cast to the earth, and his angels were cast out with him. (Revelations 12:7–9)

Note: This scripture does not say fallen angels were cast into hell and chained as it does in 2 Peter 2:4.

e)   He is a military leader, head of the warrior angels.
f)   He stands up for God's people and opposes God's enemies.
g)   He is always defending, fighting, or aiding others.
h)   Michael the archangel is always mentioned with respect and admiration by those that saw him in the Bible.

5.   Gabriel—Daniel 8–9; Luke 1

Then it happened, when I, Daniel, had seen the vision and was seeking the meaning, that suddenly there stood before me one having the appearance of a man. And I heard a *man's voice* between the banks of the Ulai, who called, and said, "Gabriel, make this man understand the vision." So, he came near where I stood, and when he came, I was afraid and fell on my face; but he said to me, "Understand, son of man, that the vision refers to the time of the end."

Now, as he was speaking with me, I was in a deep sleep with my face to the ground; but he touched me, and stood me upright. And he said, "Look, I am making known to you what shall happen in the latter time of the indignation; for at the appointed time the end shall be. The ram which you saw, having the two horns—they are the kings of Media and Persia. And the male goat is the kingdom of Greece. The large horn that is between its eyes is the first king. As for the broken horn and the four that stood up in its place, four kingdoms shall arise out of that nation, but not with its power. (Daniel 8:15–22)

a)   He is the highest-ranking messenger angel and the only other angel mentioned by name in the Bible.
b)   He communicates God's messages for His purposes.
c)   He appeared as a man, had a voice like a man, had power of touch like humans.
d)   He has great strength and swift speed.
e)   Gabriel means "man of God."
f)   Tradition says that he was an archangel, but the Bible is not specific about this.
g)   He is an important messenger angel that, according to Luke 1:19, stands in the presence of God. The angel was speaking to Joseph, concerning Mary and the birth of Jesus.

And the angel answered and said to him, "I am Gabriel, who stands in the presence of God, and was sent to speak to you and bring you these glad tidings. But behold, you will be mute and not able to speak until the day these things take place, because you did not believe my words which will be fulfilled in their own time." (Luke 1:19)

h)   Gabriel appears in the Bible four times.
i)   Each time he appears, he is announcing God's plan and purpose concerning Jesus and the end-times.

j) Daniel had an encounter with Gabriel in his second vision from God.

Then it happened, when I, Daniel, had seen the vision and was seeking the meaning, that suddenly there stood before me one having the appearance of a man. And I heard a man's voice between the banks of the Ulai, who called, and said, "Gabriel, make this man understand the vision." So, he came near where I stood, and when he came, I was afraid and fell on my face; but he said to me, "Understand, son of man, that the vision refers to the time of the end. Now, as he was speaking with me, I was in a deep sleep with my face to the ground; but he touched me, and stood me upright." (Daniel 8:15–17)

k) Daniel had another visitation from Gabriel in Daniel 9:20–23.

Now while I was speaking, praying, and confessing my sin and the sin of my people Israel, and presenting my supplication before the Lord my God for the holy mountain of my God, yes, while I was speaking in prayer, the man Gabriel, whom I had seen in the vision at the beginning, being caused to fly swiftly, reached me about the time of the evening offering. And he informed me, and talked with me, and said, "O Daniel, I have now come forth to give you skill to understand. At the beginning of your supplications the command went out, and I have come to tell you, for you are greatly beloved; therefore, consider the matter, and understand the vision."

l) Gabriel explained to Daniel about the seventy weeks in verse 24 of Daniel 9. And in *verse 24–27*, Gabriel interpreted God's purpose and plan for the people of Israel and Jesus the Messiah. "Seventy weeks are determined."

m) For your people and for your holy city, To finish the transgression, To make an end of sins, To make reconciliation for iniquity, To bring in everlasting righteousness, To seal up vision and prophecy, And to anoint the Most Holy. "Know therefore and understand, That from the going forth of the command To restore and build Jerusalem Until Messiah the Prince, There shall be seven weeks and sixty-two weeks; The street shall be built again, and the wall, Even in troublesome times. "And after the sixty-two weeks Messiah shall be cut off, but not for Himself; And the people of the prince who is to come Shall destroy the city and the sanctuary. The end of it shall be with a flood, And till the end of the war desolations are determined. Then he shall confirm a covenant with many for one week; But in the middle of the week He shall bring an end to sacrifice and offering. And on the wing of abominations shall be one who makes desolate, Even until the consummation, which is determined, Is poured out on the desolate."

n) Gabriel also announced the birth of John the Baptist to his parents.

Then an angel of the Lord appeared to him, standing on the right side of the altar of incense. And when Zacharias saw him, he was troubled, and fear fell upon him. But the angel said to him, "Do not be afraid, Zacharias, for your prayer is heard; and your wife Elizabeth will bear you a son, and you shall call his name John." (Luke 1:11–13)

And he will turn many of the children of Israel to the Lord their God. He will also go before Him in the spirit and power of Elijah, 'to turn the hearts of the fathers to the children,' and the disobedient to the wisdom of the just, to make ready a people prepared for the Lord.

And Zacharias said to the angel, "How shall I know this? For I am an old man, and my wife is well advanced in years."

And the angel answered and said to him, "I am Gabriel, who stands in the presence of God, and was sent to speak to you and bring you these glad tidings. But behold, you will be mute and not able to speak until the day these things take place, because you did not believe my words which will be fulfilled in their own time." (Luke 1:16–19)

o)   This angel also announced the birth of Jesus.

Now in the sixth month the angel Gabriel was sent by God to a city of Galilee named Nazareth, to a virgin betrothed to a man whose name was Joseph, of the house of David. The virgin's name was Mary. And having come in, the angel said to her, "Rejoice, highly favored one, the Lord is with you; blessed are you among women!" But when she saw him, she was troubled at his saying, and considered what manner of greeting this was. Then the angel said to her, "Do not be afraid, Mary, for you have found favor with God. And behold, you will conceive in your womb and bring forth a Son and shall call His name Jesus. He will be great and will be called the Son of the Highest; and the Lord God will give Him the throne of His father David. And He will reign over the house of Jacob forever, and of His kingdom there will be no end." Then Mary said to the angel, "How can this be, since I do not know a man?" And the angel answered and said to her, "The Holy Spirit will come upon you, and the power of the Highest will overshadow you; therefore, also, that Holy One who is to be born will be called the Son of God. Now indeed, Elizabeth your relative has also conceived a son in her old age; and this is now the sixth month for her who was called barren. For with God nothing will be impossible." Then Mary said, "Behold the maidservant of the Lord! Let it be to me according to your word." And the angel departed from her. (Luke 1:26–33)

> p) Gabriel will probably be the one coming back with Jesus to get the church.

For the Lord Himself will descend from heaven with a shout, with the voice of an archangel, and with the trumpet of God. And the dead in Christ will rise first. (1 Thessalonians 4:16.)

Gabriel is God's trustworthy messenger angel who stands in His presence and brings important news to God's people.

B. Heavenly beings

1. Cherubim

The cherubim spread out their wings above, and covered the mercy seat with their wings. They faced one another; the faces of the cherubim were toward the mercy seat. (Exodus 37:9)

So, He drove out the man; and He placed cherubim at the east of the garden of Eden, and a flaming sword which turned every way, to guard the way to the tree of life. (Genesis 3:24)

> a) Highest ranking of heavenly beings
> b) Have a face and two wings
> c) They are powerful and holy beings.
> d) They were mentioned the first time in Genesis 3:24 as the angel to guard the garden of Eden and make sure Adam and Eve did not return.
> e) Angels guarded the Garden of Eden and the Tree of Life after Adam fell.
> f) Symbol on lid of ark

Who serve the copy and shadow of the heavenly things, as Moses was divinely instructed when he was about to make the tabernacle. For He said, "See that you make all things according to the pattern shown you on the mountain." (Hebrews 8:5)

g) Purpose: protect God's glory and proclaim His grace.

And you shall make two cherubim of gold; of hammered work you shall make them at the two ends of the mercy seat. Make one cherub at one end, and the other cherub at the other end; you shall make the cherubim at the two ends of it of one piece with the mercy seat. And the cherubim shall stretch out their wings above, covering the mercy seat with their wings, and they shall face one another; the faces of the cherubim shall be toward the mercy seat. You shall put the mercy seat on top of the ark, and in the ark, you shall put the Testimony that I will give you. And there I will meet with you, and I will speak with you from above the mercy seat, from between the two cherubim which are on the ark of the Testimony, about everything which I will give you in commandment to the children of Israel. (Exodus 25:18–22)

h) Cherubim is described in detail in *Ezekiel 10:1–21.*
i) Second Samuel 22:10–11 tells us that God rode upon a cherub and did fly.

He bowed the heavens also and came down. With darkness under His feet. He rode upon a cherub and flew; And He was seen upon the wings of the wind. He made darkness canopies around Him.

j) God assigned cherubim angels with special assignment that others don't have.

This tells of Lucifer's fall.

You were the anointed cherub who covers; I established you; You were on the holy mountain of God; You walked back and forth in the midst of fiery stones. You were perfect in your ways from the day you were created, Till iniquity was found in you. By the abundance of your trading You became filled with violence within, And you sinned; Therefore I cast you as a profane thing Out of the mountain of God; And I destroyed you, O covering cherub, From the midst of the fiery stones. Your heart was lifted up because of your beauty; You corrupted your wisdom for the sake of your splendor; I cast you to the ground, I laid you before kings, That they might gaze at you. You defiled your sanctuaries By the multitude of your iniquities, By the iniquity of your trading; Therefore I brought fire from your midst; It devoured you, And I turned you to ashes upon the earth In the sight of all who saw you. All who knew you among the peoples are astonished at you; You have become a horror, And shall be no more forever.(Ezekiel 28:14–19)

k)   There are seven separate places in the Bible where we can read that our Lord is the God who "dwells between the cherubim."

    a)   So, the people sent to Shiloh, that they might bring from there the ark of the covenant of the Lord of hosts, who dwells between the cherubim. And the two sons of Eli, Hophni and Phinehas, were there with the ark of the covenant of God. (1 Samuel 4:4)

    b)   And David arose and went with all the people who were with him from Baale Judah to bring up from there the ark of God, whose name is called by the Name, the Lord of

Hosts, who dwells between the cherubim.
(2 Samuel 6:2)

c)   Then Hezekiah prayed before the Lord, and
said: "O Lord God of Israel, the One who
dwells between the cherubim, you are God,
You alone, of all the kingdoms of the earth. You
have made heaven and earth. (2 Kings 19:15)

d)   And David and all Israel went up to Baalah, to
Kirjath Jearim, which belonged to Judah, to
bring up from there the ark of God the Lord,
who dwells between the cherubim, where His
name is proclaimed. (1 Chronicles 13:6)

e)   Give ear, O Shepherd of Israel You who lead
Joseph like a flock; You who dwell between
the cherubim, shine forth! (Psalm 80:1)

f)   The Lord reigns; Let the people's tremble!
He dwells between the cherubim; Let the
earth be moved! (Psalm 99:1)

g)   O Lord of hosts, God of Israel, the One who
dwells between the cherubim, you are God,
You alone, of all the kingdoms of the earth. You
have made heaven and earth. (Isaiah 37:16)

l)   Two scriptures that tell us the Lord rode upon
their wings.

He rode upon a cherub and flew; and He was seen
upon the wings of the wind. (2 Samuel 22:11)

And He rode upon a cherub and flew;
He flew upon the wings of the wind. (Psalm
18:10)

2.   Seraphim

In the year that King Uzziah died, I saw the Lord sitting on a throne, high and lifted up, and the train of His robe filled the temple. Above it stood seraphim; each one had six wings: with two he covered his face, with two he covered his feet, and with two he flew. And one cried to another and said: "Holy, holy, holy is the Lord of hosts; The whole earth is full of His glory!" And the posts of the door were shaken by the voice of him who cried out, and the house was filled with smoke. So I said: "Woe is me, for I am undone! Because I am a man of unclean lips, And I dwell in the midst of a people of unclean lips; For my eyes have seen the King, The Lord of hosts." Then one of the seraphim flew to me, having in his hand a live coal which he had taken with the tongs from the altar. And he touched my mouth with it, and said: "Behold, this has touched your lips; Your iniquity is taken away, and your sin purged." Also I heard the voice of the Lord, saying: (Isaiah 6:1–8)

a)   They have six wings, two covered face, two covered feet, and two that help them fly.
b)   They hover above and on each side of God's throne.

They are only mentioned once in the Bible where Isaiah described them in detail (Isaiah 6:1–8).

c)   Their purpose is to show the holiness of God.
d)   In the Hebrew, Seraphim means "burning ones."
e)   They have great power in their voices.
f)   There is nothing weak about these creatures.
g)   Then another angel, having a golden censer, came and stood at the altar. He was given much incense, that he should offer it with the prayers

of all the saints upon the golden altar which was before the throne. And the smoke of the incense, with the prayers of the saints, ascended before God from the angel's hand. Then the angel took the censer, filled it with fire from the altar, and threw it to the earth. And there were noises, thunderings, lightnings, and an earthquake. So the seven angels who had the seven trumpets prepared themselves to sound. (Revelation 8:3–5)

h) God used a seraphim to cleanse Isaiah's communication.

i) Seraphim are closer to their Creator than all the other angels, hovering above the throne of God.

j) In Isaiah 6:5–7, a seraphim was sent by God to touch Isaiah's mouth and purify it with live coals from the altar of heaven.

I said:

"Woe is me, for I am undone Because I am a man of unclean lips, And I dwell in the midst of a people of unclean lips;

For my eyes have seen the King, The Lord of hosts."

Then one of the seraphim flew to me, having in his hand a live coal which he had taken with the tongs from the altar. And he touched my mouth with it, and said: "Behold, this has touched your lips; Your iniquity is taken away, and your sin purged." (Isaiah 6:5–7)

3. Living creatures (Ezekiel 1, Revelation 4–5)

a) They have four faces, four wings, and a hand under each wing.

b) Their purpose is to worship God directly, witness worship of God by believers and direct judgments of God.

c) Could be either cherubim or seraphim instead of a class of their own.

4.   Guardian angels

I saw in the visions of my head while on my bed, and there was a watcher, a holy one, coming down from heaven. He cried aloud and said thus: "This decision is by the decree of the watchers. And the sentence by the word of the holy ones, In order that the living may know That the Most High rules in the kingdom of men, Gives it to whomever He will, And sets over it the lowest of men." And inasmuch as the king saw a watcher, a holy one, coming down from heaven and saying, "Chop down the tree and destroy it, but leave its stump and roots in the earth, bound with a band of iron and bronze in the tender grass of the field; let it be wet with the dew of heaven, and let him graze with the beasts of the field, till seven times pass over him"; (Daniel 4:13, 17, 23)

a)   One who has care of a person or property of another, a protector, to protector from danger and to preserve.

b)   We could call them our special secret service that are here assigned to deliver us from evil plots of the enemy.

c)   The angel of the Lord encamps all around those who fear Him and delivers them. (Psalm 34:7)

d)   He delivers me from my enemies. You also lift me up above those who rise against me; You have delivered me from the violent man. (Psalm 18:48)

e)   Jacob declares that the angel assigned to him had redeemed and delivered him from all evil. Jacob had a guardian angel, just like you and me. His angel was with him his whole life, just as your angel is with you your whole life.

The Angel who has redeemed me from all evil, Bless the lads; Let my name be named upon them, And the name of my fathers Abraham and

Isaac; And let them grow into a multitude in the midst of the earth. (Genesis 48:16)

    f)   Guardian angels have charge over you.

With long life I will satisfy him and show him My salvation. (Psalm 91:11–16)

    g)   Long life and guardian angels go hand in hand.
    h)   I, Jesus, have sent My angel to testify to you these things in the churches. I am the Root and the Offspring of David, the Bright and Morning Star. (Revelations 22:16)
    i)   This was probably Peter's personal angel, and when he went to John Mark's house, those praying declared it was *his* angel. By this statement, we can assume and believe the early church must have had New Testament teaching and sound doctrine concerning angels and their assignment.

Peter was therefore kept in prison, but constant prayer was offered to God for him by the church. And when Herod was about to bring him out, that night Peter was sleeping, bound with two chains between two soldiers; and the guards before the door were keeping the prison. Now behold, an angel of the Lord stood by him, and a light shone in the prison; and he struck Peter on the side and raised him up, saying, "Arise quickly!" And his chains fell off his hands. Then the angel said to him, "Gird yourself and tie on your sandals"; and so, he did. And he said to him, "Put on your garment and follow me." So, he went out and followed him, and did not know that what was done by the angel was real, but thought he was seeing a vision. When they were past the first and the second guard posts, they came to the iron gate that leads to the city, which opened to them of its own accord; and they went out and went down one street, and immediately the angel departed from him. And when Peter had come to himself, he said, "Now I know for certain that the Lord has sent His angel, and has delivered me from the hand of Herod and from all the expectation of the Jewish people." So, when he had considered this, he came to the house of Mary, the mother of John whose surname was Mark, where many were gathered together praying. And as Peter knocked at the door of the gate, a girl named Rhoda came to answer. When she recognized Peter's voice, because of her gladness she did not open the gate, but ran in and announced that Peter stood before the gate. But they said to her, "You are beside yourself!" Yet she kept insisting that it was so. So, they said, "It is his angel." Now Peter continued knocking; and when they opened the door and saw him, they were astonished. (Acts 12:5–15)

5.   Angels—hosts, stars

His tail drew a third of the stars of heaven and threw them to the earth. And the dragon stood before the woman who was ready to give birth, to devour her Child as soon as it was born. (Revelation 12:4)

a)   Chief assignment of all ranking, good angels is to praise and worship God.
b)   Highest- to the lowest-ranking good angels.
c)   They are dispatched by higher ranking to help us, minister to us.
d)   Angels reveal things to us
e)   Angels guide us
f)   Angels provide for us
g)   Angels protect us
h)   Angels deliver us from situations
i)   Angels strengthen us
j)   Angels encourage us
k)   Angels assist in answering Prayers
l)   Angels will escort us to heaven at death

Things angels cannot do

      a)   Call God "Father," only Creator
      b)   Preach the gospel, only humans can do that
      c)   Be redeemed or conformed to image of Christ
      d)   Indwell man (only Holy Spirit can do that)
      e)   Act on their own power or out of their own will
      f)   Become human beings (can appear as men but not be them). Angels are not glorified human beings.

6.   Guardian angels

Take heed that you do not despise one of these little ones, for I say to you that in heaven their angels always see the face of My Father who is in heaven. For the Son of Man has come to save that which was lost. (Matthew 18:10)

7.   In Acts 12, you will find that:
      a.   Angels are assigned at birth.
      b.   Individuals, churches, nations can have guardian angels.
      c.   Chief angel who escorts believers to heaven at death.

CHAPTER 5

Lucifer/Satan

I. The questions for this study and topic concerning Lucifer would be, do you believe in his existence, and how does he effect the plan God has for man? Here are a few things to think about as we do a short study of Lucifer and his followers, better known as fallen angels.

    A. A poll done in the US showed that 49 percent of Americans believe that evil angels exist.

    B. The other 50 percent believed either there are no supernatural beings or that there are no evil ones, only good angels.

    C. In another study, some believers said they believe bad angels exist, but only good ones could influence someone's life.

    D. Unfortunately, belief does not make anything true or false.

    E. Your belief will influence the way you deal with truth or falsehood.

    F. The question is, does Satan exist? What do you believe?

    G. Here are some biblical facts to help us be assured Satan does exist and is at work in this world to kill, steal, and destroy our lives.

        1. There are seven books in the Old Testament that refer to Satan.

        2. Every book in the New Testament refers to Satan by their writers.

3. There are twenty-nine specific references to Satan in the New Testament, and Jesus Himself is speaking in twenty-five of these scriptures.

I think we can safely say that to reject something that Jesus Himself accepted as true, this includes the belief in angels, would be to deny the authority of the Bible itself and a personal attack on the Lord Jesus Himself.

H. It is important to understand that Satan is real and that he is the father of all lies, and there is no truth in him.
I. He is not just evil but he is the very essence of evil.
J. He was and is the first sinner and father of all sin.
K. One Bible scholar by the name Chafer wrote, "The fall of this mighty angel was not a compromise between good and evil. He became the embodiment of evil and wholly void of good."
L. Never should we elevate him to the same level as God.
M. He was a created being by God Himself for the sole purpose of worshipping Him.
N. God is all-knowing, but Satan is not.
O. God knows your future, but Satan does not.
P. When we act in the flesh, "which he controls," he can predict our future! Then he can influence and predict the outcome of our lives if we continue acting and operating in the flesh.
Q. The redeemed nature of man is something Satan has never understood. And when we let the Holy Spirit lead our lives, Satan has no control or influence in our lives.
R. Based on Ezekiel 28:14–19, I believe Lucifer was created as cherubim.

II. Lucifer and the angelic rebellion

He was once called the "son of the morning."

He may have been an archangel, like Michael, but was thrown out of heaven when he rebelled. He and his fallen angels that fell with him continue to fight and be a nuisance in the world today.

Scripture does not back up the theory that Satan was an arch-angel even though some scholars and bible teachers teach that he was an archangel.

In 2 Thessalonians 2:7, Paul calls it the mystery of iniquity! Why did Satan and his army rebel in the first place?

They fell because they sinned against God.

> For if God did not spare the angels who sinned but cast them down to hell and delivered them into chains of darkness, to be reserved for judgment. (2 Peter 2:4)

The Bible is not specific in when this happened. But scholars agree it was between the creation and Satan's intrusion in the garden of Eden, between Genesis 1:1 and 1:2.

I believe God created the angels before the seven days of creation in Genesis, and they were good until sometime after the seven days of creation. God said everything was good at the end of his six days of work and rested on the seventh.

All unrighteousness and transgressions against God can be described as self-willed against the will of God.

This applies to humans today as well as angels.

All angels were created to worship God and to glorify Him. But Lucifer wanted supreme authority for himself, and thus we have the angels being kicked out of heaven as one-third of the angelic forces rebelled with Satan. *Isaiah 14* tells us why Satan fell and what he wanted.

Satan used deception to cause the angels to rebel and follow him, just as he does today with humans.

> How you are fallen from heaven, O Lucifer, son of the morning! How you are cut down to the ground, You who weakened the nations! For you have said in your heart: I will ascend into heaven, I will exalt my throne above the stars of God; I will also sit on the mount of the congregation On the farthest sides of the north; I will ascend above the heights of the clouds, I will be like the Most High. Yet you shall be brought down to Sheol, To the lowest depths of the Pit. (Isaiah 14:12–15)

A. Son of man, take up a lamentation for the king of Tyre, and say to him, `Thus says the Lord GOD: "You were the seal of perfection, Full of wisdom and perfect in beauty. You were in Eden, the garden of God; Every precious stone was your covering: The sardius, topaz, and diamond, Beryl, onyx, and jasper, Sapphire, turquoise, and emerald with gold. The workmanship of your timbrels and pipes Was prepared for you on the day you were created. *"You were the anointed cherub who covers; I established you; You were on the holy mountain of God; You walked back and forth in the midst of fiery stones. You were perfect in your ways from the day you were created, till iniquity was found in you.* "By the abundance of your trading You became filled with violence within, and you sinned; therefore, I cast you as a profane thing Out of the mountain of God; And I destroyed you, O covering cherub, From the midst of the fiery stones. "Your heart was lifted up because of your beauty; You corrupted your wisdom for the sake of your splendor; I cast you to the ground, I laid you before kings, that they might gaze at you. "You defiled your sanctuaries by the multitude of your iniquities, By the iniquity of your trading; therefore, I brought fire from your midst; It devoured you, And I turned you to ashes upon the earth in the sight of all who saw you. All who knew you among the peoples are astonished at you; You have become a horror and shall be no more forever." (Ezekiel 28:12–19)

1. *Verse 12* is a detailed picture of beauty and wisdom with which he was created (full of wisdom, perfect in beauty, perfect in his ways).
2. *Verse 13* says all music came through him in perfect harmony, commissioned by God to minister to Him and cover His glory with music through praise and worship.
3. *Verse 14* talks about anointed cherub, the highest angel of God's creation, high official with authority and responsibility to protect and defend.
4. *Verse 17* says he became prideful.

B.   Fall of Lucifer

How you are fallen from heaven, O Lucifer, son of the morning! How you are cut down to the ground, you who weakened the nations! For you have said in your heart: 'I will ascend into heaven, I will exalt my throne above the stars of God; I will also sit on the mount of the congregation On the farthest sides of the north; I will ascend above the heights of the clouds, I will be like the Most High.' Yet you shall be brought down to Sheol, To the lowest depths of the Pit. "Those who see you will gaze at you, and consider you, saying: 'Is this the man who made the earth tremble, who shook kingdoms, Who made the world as a wilderness and destroyed its cities, who did not open the house of his prisoners?'" (Isaiah 14:12–17)

1.   *Verse 13–14* states that pride led him to lift his will above God.

   a)   "I will ascend into heaven, I will exalt my throne above the stars of God, I will sit on the mount of congregation on sides of north, I will ascend above heights of the clouds."
   b)   "I will be like the most high."

2.   Pride and self will lead to rebellion.

   a)   Lucifer was cast out of heaven and the office he held, with one-third of the angels who followed him.

And war broke out in heaven: Michael and his angels fought with the dragon; and the dragon and his angels fought, but they did not prevail, nor was a place found for them in heaven any longer. So, the great dragon was cast out, that serpent of old, called the Devil and Satan, who deceives the whole world; he was cast to the earth, and his angels were cast out with him. (Revelation 12:7–9)

       b)   When he fell from heaven, he became known as Satan, our adversary.

C.   Satan and fallen angels now dwell in our atmosphere.

    1.   Satan is not in hell.
    2.   Satan has access to third heaven.

Now there was a day when the sons of God came to present themselves before the Lord, and Satan also came among them. And the Lord said to Satan, "From where do you come?" So Satan answered the Lord and said, "From going to and fro on the earth, and from walking back and forth on it." (Job 1:6)

III. Satan

A.   Evil is simply a perversion of something that was originally good.

    1.   Satan cannot create anything, only pervert, distort, copy, and destroy.
    2.   His power is limited to what was given him when he was created. He perverts that power to build his ego and use for his purposes.

B.   His position over music was not taken from him, but he corrupted it.

    1.   That is why worldly music is violent and sensual but affects human beings.
    2.   He still has power to create worship but uses it to worship himself.
    3.   The church replaces him in giving worship and praise to God.
    4.   His main sphere of operation is in the earth.

Job 1:7; So, Satan answered the Lord and said, "From going to and fro on the earth, and from walking back and forth on it." (Job 1:7)

5. He influences governments to make laws and allow things to oppose God.
6. He sets up substitutes for God (money, power, position, etc.).

C. His names in the Bible and their meanings: There are at least forty different names that Satan is called throughout the Bible.

1. Devil—slanderer, accuser, prince of demons
2. Serpent—deceiver, crafty
3. Abaddon, which means destroyer
4. Great dragon, which speaks of his perverted power (destructive beast)
5. Beelzebub—prince of demons; "lord of the flies," changed by Jews to mean "lord of the dunghill" where flies like to congregate.

A disciple is not above his teacher, nor a servant above his master. It is enough for a disciple that he be like his teacher, and a servant like his master. If they have called the master of the house Beelzebub, how much more will they call those of his household! Therefore, do not fear them. For there is nothing covered that will not be revealed and hidden that will not be known. (Matthew 10:25)

6. Belial—worthless, tempter, gets men to sin
7. Wicked, evil, lawless one—His ways are wicked.
8. Prince of this world, which speaks of his rule and influence over governments of the world
9. God of this world—rulership of religion
10. Deceiver or accuser
11. Angel of light—poses as spiritual helper to lead those who need help out of their darkness.

12. Murderer—tempting men to sin, promoting death
13. Father of lies—cannot speak truth
14. Roaring lion—false fierceness and strength
15. Destroyer—angel of bottomless pit
16. The evil one
17. Liar: father of lies
18. Wicked, lawless one
19. As a roaring lion
20. Anointed cherub "who covers"
21. Lucifer, "son of the morning"

In *Ephesians 6:12*, prince of the power of the air is suggesting his rulership over the fallen angels and that there is a highly organized army behind all the evil in this world's system.

> For we do not wrestle against flesh and blood, but against principalities, against powers, against the rulers of the darkness of this age, against spiritual hosts of wickedness in the heavenly places.

D. During the millennium, Satan will be chained in the bottomless pit, he will be released for a time, then he will be judged by God and thrown into the lake of fire for eternity.

CHAPTER 6

Fallen Angels/Demons

There are two equal and opposite errors into which
our race can fall about the devils (demons). One
is to disbelieve their existence, The other is to
believe and feel an unhealthy interest in them

—C. S. Lewis

If angels are real, if we believe that the angels of God and evil angels exist, and if the devil is real, then demons must also exist. One question that has always existed and still does today: Are fallen angels and demons the same being? There are different opinions concerning this, and we will spend a little time discussing it in this study. There are many questions concerning demons: What do they look like? Are they like men, animals, half men, and half animals? Are they male or female? According to the Bible there is only one devil but there can be many fallen angels and legions of demons. The origin of demons is more of a mystery than that of angels and Satan. Nowhere in scripture does it tell us specifically where they came from, what they look like or when they originated. Demons cannot just be a figure of speech because they are treated as realities in the Bible and particularly by Jesus Himself.

Example: If a legion was a figure of speech, it could not cause a herd of pigs to self-destruct (Mark 5:1–13).

Then they sailed to the country of the
Gadarenes, which is opposite Galilee. And when

He stepped out on the land, there met Him a certain man from the city who had demons for a long time. And he wore no clothes, nor did he live in a house but in the tombs. When he saw Jesus, he cried out, fell down before Him, and with a loud voice said, "What have I to do with You, Jesus, Son of the Most High God? I beg You, do not torment me!" For He had commanded the unclean spirit to come out of the man. For it had often seized him, and he was kept under guard, bound with chains and shackles; and he broke the bonds and was driven by the demon into the wilderness.

Jesus asked him, saying, "What is your name?"

And he said, "Legion," because many demons had entered him. And they begged Him that He would not command them to go out into the abyss. Now a herd of many swine was feeding there on the mountain. So, they begged Him that He would permit them to enter them. And He permitted them. Then the demons went out of the man and entered the swine, and the herd ran violently down the steep place into the lake and drowned. (Luke 8:26–33)

One thing we can be sure of, at some point, demons, as they are called today, were created, and God is the only Creator. They must have been created good and, at some point, must have rebelled against God.

There are four main theories concerning where demons came from. There may be more, but the four listed below are the four principal ones that I have found. These four descriptions were taken from Terry Law's book, *The Truth about Angels*. I agree with his rendering and description.

1. Demons are disembodied inhabitants of a preadamite earth. This perspective is based on the gap theory. According to this theory, the world that was created before Adam was under Lucifer's rule. When Lucifer fell, the inhabitants of

this world rebelled against God as well. These rebellious spirits are the demons that operate in the world today.

2. Demons are the offspring of angels and woman who came together before the flood. The offspring were destroyed in the flood, but their spirits remained on earth as demons.

> Now it came to pass, when men began to multiply on the face of the earth, and daughters were born to them, that the sons of God saw the daughters of men, that they were beautiful; and they took wives for themselves of all whom they chose. And the Lord said, "My Spirit shall not strive with man forever, for he is indeed flesh; yet his days shall be one hundred and twenty years." There were giants on the earth in those days, and also afterward, when the sons of God came into the daughters of men, and they bore children to them. Those were the mighty men who were of old, men of renown. (Genesis 6:1–4)

3. Demons are the offspring of the sons of Seth and the daughters of Cain. This is a variation of theory number two. Its main weakness is that everywhere else in the Old Testament where the term "sons of God" is used; it refers to angels (*Genesis 6:1–4*).

4. Demons are fallen angels. This theory comes from the number of scriptures that refer to a great host of spirits designated as under the authority of Satan, Beelzebub, or the prince of demons.

> If Satan casts out Satan, he is divided against himself. How then will his kingdom stand? And if I cast out demons by Beelzebub, by whom do your sons cast them out? Therefore, they shall be your judges. (Matthew 12:26–27)

Why some of these fallen angels would be cast down to hell or kept in chains of darkness and others left free is not made clear if this is the correct theory.

> And the angels who did not keep their
> proper domain, but left their own abode, He has
> reserved in everlasting chains under darkness for
> the judgment of the great day. (Jude 1:6)

Even if we cannot agree and if their origin is uncertain, we can all agree and know for certain that demons exist and are active in this world today. They are active in keeping people from trusting in Jesus and His plan for redemption. Demons are constantly working in people's lives to destroy them and hinder them from serving God.

I personally believe in the first theory that demons came from the preadamite race. We know there were people here before Adam because God told Adam to go and replenish the earth. To replenish means there had to be something here before Adam existed.

> And God blessed them, and God said unto
> them, be fruitful, and multiply, *and replenish the
> earth*, and subdue it: and have dominion over
> the fish of the sea, and over the fowl of the air,
> and over every living thing that moveth upon the
> earth. (Genesis 1:28 KJV)

One thing to consider in this theory is the fact that demons desire to inhabit or be embodied in human beings and sometimes animals.

Fallen angels already have a body! So it doesn't make sense that they desire to inhabit someone else's body.

Whichever theory you choose to believe is okay with me. It has nothing to do with redemption and your salvation or relationship to our Lord Jesus Christ.

I.   Hierarchy of evil angels

    A.   They are placed over nations as some good angels are placed over nations.

    B.   When Christians pray for their nations, take authority, and speak the Word, good angels prevail; when they do not, evil angels prevail.

II. Demons—working class of evil angels

   A. There is one devil, many fallen angels, and multitudes of demons.

   B. The Bible does not specifically tell what demons are or where or when they originated.

   C. Theories where demons came from

      1. Preadamite earth

         a) Involved with Genesis gap theory
         b) There was a world created before Adam under Lucifer's rule.
         c) When Lucifer fell and came to earth, the inhabitants of the world under the influence of Lucifer rebelled against God also.
         d) These spirits from the rebellious inhabitants of earth are the demons today.

      2. Offspring of angels (sons of God) and women (daughters of men) (*Genesis 6:1–2, 4*). The offspring of the union of these two classes were destroyed in Noah's flood, but the spirits remain on earth as demons.

      3. Fallen angels

         a) Demons look for bodies to inhabit.
         b) Fallen angels already have bodies and are not looking for ones to inhabit.

   D. Purpose of fallen angels and demons

      1. Twofold: to hinder the purposes of God, to carry out the purposes of Satan

      2. To fulfill these two purposes, they do the following:

         a) Keep people from trusting God
         b) Pull Christians into error
         c) Hinder Christians from being victorious

E.   Nature/character of fallen angels and demons

1.   They have names just as good angels.

> And Jesus asked him, saying, what is thy name? And he said, Legion: because many devils were entered into him. (Luke 8:30)

2.   They speak and hear as good angels do.
3.   They have intelligence as good angels do.
4.   Demons exercise their wills.

> And there was there a herd of many swine feeding on the mountain: and they besought him that he would suffer them to enter into them. And he suffered them. (Luke 8:32)

5.   They have emotions as good angels do.

> And when he went forth to land, there met him out of the city a certain man, which had devils long time, and ware no clothes, neither abode in any house, but in the tombs. When he saw Jesus, he cried out, and fell down before him, and with a loud voice said, what have I to do with thee, Jesus, thou Son of God most high? I beseech thee, torment me not. (Luke 8:27–28 KJV)

> Thou believest that there is one God; thou doest well: the devils also believe, and tremble. (James 2:19 KJV)

6.   They crave attention like Satan, opposite of good angels.

a)   Emphasizing them seems to attract them to a person.
b)   It is best not to spend a lot of time talking about them or giving them attention. Deal with them when necessary, but primary focus should stay on Jesus.

7. They cannot be in more than one place at a time.
8. They can have supernatural strength.
9. They can cause various physical ailments and afflictions.

    a) Dumbness, deafness
    b) Blindness
    c) Insanity
    d) Suicide
    e) Personal injury
    f) Various defects and deformities
    g) Spirit of Infirmity

10. They can possess people.
11. They feel comforted when they are embodied. They like living in the soul, flesh, or spirit of human beings.
12. They are shrewd and knowledgeable about human nature.
13. They can adapt to cultural environment of a place or age.

F. Two specific evil angels that we will discuss:

> I am he that liveth, and was dead; and behold, I am alive for evermore, Amen; and have the keys of hell and of death. (Revelations 1:18)

1. Death has power over people's bodies and power to induce physical death.
2. Hades presides over the place of the dead where the wicked are being held with pending judgment.

> And I saw a great white throne, and him that sat on it, from whose face the earth and the heaven fled away; and there was found no place for them. And I saw the dead, small and great, stand before God; and the books were opened: and another book was opened, which is the book of life: and the dead were judged out of those things which were written in the books, according to their works. And the sea gave up the dead which were in it; and death and hell delivered

up the dead which were in them: and they were judged every man according to their works. And death and hell were cast into the lake of fire. This is the second death. And whosoever was not found written in the book of life was cast into the lake of fire. (Revelation 20:11–15)

CHAPTER 7

Spiritual Warfare

I.   What is true warfare?

A.   True warfare occurs when we exalt Jesus in righteousness and faith.

B.   Nowhere in the Bible are we told to fight the devil.

    1.   Jesus did that once and for all on the cross.

    2.   We know Jesus went to hell for three days when He died to pay the penalty for us who deserved to go to hell.

    3.   When he ascended on high, he led captives in his train… (Ephesians 4:8)

        a)   He ascended after He descended into hell.

        b)   When ascending into the third heaven, He passed through the second heaven.

    4.   And having disarmed the powers and authorities, he made a public spectacle of them, triumphing over them by the cross. (Colossians 2:15)

        a)   Disarmed—a military ceremony when a victorious Roman general would stand before a defeated general in the presence of both armies. He would strip the defeated general of all symbols of authority—metals, badges, insignia—and would also strip him of all his military names and titles and claim them for his own.

b) Jesus stripped Satan of all his power that God had given him when he was created. Any authority Satan once had now belonged to Jesus.

C. If Satan is defeated, then so are his angels.

1. I am the Living One; I was dead, and behold I am alive for ever and ever! And I hold the keys of Death and Hades. (Revelations1:18)

2. Remember, Death and Hades are names of two evil angels.

3. In the Bible, to have keys means having authority!

4. Jesus took the authority from the angels who oversaw death and hell.

D. Then Jesus came to them and said, "All authority in heaven and on earth has been given to me. (Matthew 28:18)

1. When He defeated Satan, He delegated His authority immediately to the church.

And he said unto them, go ye into all the world, and preach the gospel to every creature. He that believeth and is baptized shall be saved; but he that believeth not shall be damned. And these signs shall follow them that believe; In my name shall they cast out devils; they shall speak with new tongues; They shall take up serpents; and if they drink any deadly thing, it shall not hurt them; they shall lay hands on the sick, and they shall recover. (Mark 16:15–18)

But ye shall receive power, after that the Holy Ghost is come upon you: and ye shall be witnesses unto me both in Jerusalem,

and in all Judaea, and in Samaria, and unto
the uttermost part of the earth. (Acts 1:8)

2. And God raised us up with Christ and seated us with
    him in the heavenly realms in Christ Jesus. (If we are
    seated with Him in heavenly realms, then we are far
    above principalities and powers.) (Ephesians 2:6)

3. We are to speak the Word by faith against Satan and
    stand in Jesus's victory.

    a) Submit yourselves, then, to God. Resist the devil,
        and he will flee from you. (James 4:7)

        So, let God work his will in you.
        Yell a loud no to the Devil and watch
        him scamper. Say a quiet yes to God
        and he'll be there in no time. Quit
        dabbling in sin. Purify your inner life.
        Quit playing the field. Hit bottom and
        cry your eyes out. The fun and games
        are over. Get serious, really serious.
        Get down on your knees before the
        Master; it's the only way you'll get on
        your feet. (MSG)

    b) Resist him, standing firm in the faith. (1 Peter 5:9)

        Be sober [well balanced and
        self-disciplined], be alert and cautious
        at all times. That enemy of yours, the
        devil, prowls around like a roaring lion
        [fiercely hungry], seeking someone
        to devour. But resist him, be firm in
        your faith [against his attack—rooted,
        established, immovable], knowing
        that the same experiences of suffering
        are being experienced by your brothers
        and sisters throughout the world. [You
        do not suffer alone.] (AMP)

       c)   We are to have faith in Jesus's victory over the devil and faith in God's promises in the Bible

II. *The Bible reveals there are territorial spirits over nations, cities, etc. (Daniel 10).*

    A. Why are powers of darkness ruling in so many countries? Because the systems of those countries are Satan's territories, and Christians are not walking in enough light of the Word to transform those territories for Jesus by following (what is said in) *Mark 16:15–19.*

> Go into all the world and preach the gospel to every creature. He who believes and is baptized will be saved; but he who does not believe will be condemned. And these signs will follow those who believe: In My name they will cast out demons; they will speak with new tongues; they will take up serpents; and if they drink anything deadly, it will by no means hurt them; they will lay hands on the sick, and they will recover. (Mark 16:15–19 NKJ)

    B. Why are powers of darkness ruling over so many believers' lives if they have been defeated? Because they are not exercising authority even if they know they have it.

III. Our knowledge of our authority affects both good and evil angels because both operate under and respond to authority.

    A. Authority = right to rule; power = strength or force involved in enforcing authority
    B. All the universe runs under the authority principle.
    C. Jesus is high above all, and God's and Satan's angels are under His authority.
    D. Satan rules his kingdom of angels with an iron rod.

        1. Each demon knows what area he is responsible for: lust, lying, stealing, etc.

2. There is no division in Satan's kingdom.

    a) One evil spirit does not work against another.
    b) But they do not work together in love and cooperation either.
    c) They obey their authority because they must. They have no choice.

E. Evil spirits know if a person is walking in authority of God's Word and will not obey anyone who is not (is know as Sons of Sceva). (Reference is found in Acts 19:11–20).

F. If we want to operate in authority, we must come under authority.

G. There are six levels of authority:

1. Will of God
2. Truth of God's word
3. Our conscience
4. Laws of the land and church when they do not conflict with the three listed above
5. Mutual agreements (contracts)
6. Tradition when it does not conflict with above levels

H. We need to crucify wrong attitudes of our hearts so authority can operate through us. People who do not accept rightful authority over them will not be successful in taking authority over sickness or disease or casting out devils.

IV. Angels and our thoughts:

A. Every action begins with a thought.
B. Demons influence thoughts for bad, and good angels for good.
C. Demons can also push thoughts out of our minds

> When anyone hears the word of the kingdom, and does not understand it, then the wicked one comes and snatches away what was sown in his heart. This is he who received seed by the wayside. (Matthew 13:19)

> When anyone hears the word of the
> kingdom, and does not understand it, then
> the wicked one comes and snatches away
> what was sown in his heart. This is he who
> received seed by the wayside. (MSG)

Example: When reading the Bible, have you found your mind wandering? That could be because a demon is trying to get your mind off the Word and into worry, concern, or things that do not matter.

D. An undisciplined thought life opens the door to the enemy to drop in wrong thoughts. A disciplined mind is stayed on the Word (many doctors agree that 70-80 percent of all diseases originate in the mind).

E. Demons fool us into thinking the thoughts they are putting there are our own.

F. Not all thoughts come from angels.

1. Some thoughts are our carnal thoughts, and some are influenced by the world.

2. Example: Lust of sex, food, drink, gambling, love of money, desire for material possessions

V. How to operate in spiritual warfare

A. We can push back the influence of darkness in prayer so the Word can prevail in people's hearts and lives through preaching the gospel.

B. It helps to know what territorial spirits are over an area so we can find the right scriptures to pray against its thought system.

C. Territorial spirits have a lot to do with the way things are in a specific area.

D. What to pray for:

1. Your country

> If My people who are called by
> My name will humble themselves, and
> pray and seek My face, and turn from

their wicked ways, then I will hear from heaven, and will forgive their sin and heal their land. (2 Chronicles 7:14)

And my people, my God-defined people, respond by humbling themselves, praying, seeking my presence, and turning their backs on their wicked lives, I'll be there ready for you: I'll listen from heaven, forgive their sins, and restore their land to health. (MSG)

2. Those in authority

For kings and all who are in authority, that we may lead a quiet and peaceable life in all godliness and reverence. 1 Timothy 2:2 NKJ.
Pray especially for rulers and their governments to rule well so we can be quietly about our business of living simply, in humble contemplation. (1 Timothy2:2) MSG

3. People's hearts to open to the gospel; laborer's to be sent to the lost; to witness so they may be saved.

CHAPTER 8

Healing and Angels

As I began to study about angels and the part they play in our lives, I realized that angels can and do play a part in healing. We find throughout scriptures where demons caused sickness, disease, infirmities, and lifelong afflictions.

It only makes sense if fallen angels can cause sickness and disease, then heavenly angels should and do bring healing to us. Angels do not heal themselves, but they can bring healing to us in many different forms. We find many scriptures where angels that are messengers bring deliverance and strength in times of need.

We have already discussed at length the scriptures in *Hebrew 1:14 and 2:3* that tell us that angels are messengers from God. They are not the healer; Jesus is the healer. They are just the messenger that will sometimes bring healing.

> But to which of the angels has He ever said:
> "Sit at My right hand,
> Till I make Your enemies Your footstool"?
> *Are they not all ministering spirits sent forth*
> *to minister for those who will inherit salvation?*
> (Hebrews 1:13–14)

> Therefore, we must give the more earnest heed to the things we have heard, lest we drift away. *For if the word spoken through angels proved steadfast, and every transgression and disobedience received a just reward, how shall we escape if we*

neglect so great a salvation, which at the first began to be spoken by the Lord, and was confirmed to us by those who heard Him, God also bearing witness both with signs and wonders, with various miracles, and gifts of the Holy Spirit, according to His own will? (Hebrews 2:1–4)

From the beginning (with Adam and Eve) to the present time, there have continually been recorded events of miracles and supernatural healings.

Jesus Himself said greater works were coming. Angels will continue to play a significant role in the end-time harvest of souls, signs, miracles, and wonders that we will experience as we race toward the second coming of the Lord.

Quote from Roy Hicks Sr.: "If angels can strike people with sickness as they did in the Old Testament when God's judgement was carried out, then why can't angels assist with healing or removing of diseases?"

There are many testimonies and stories about how angels have brought healings or assisted with them. These events in people's lives fall into the category of extrabiblical, but they are certainly not unbiblical.

Perhaps healing is just an extension of what we have read about in scripture where people were strengthened and ministered to. Even Jesus Himself had these experiences with angels.

The best scripture to confirm that angels assist in healings is in John 5:1–4. It is evident that healing came from the direct results of an angel's participation.

After this there was a feast of the Jews, and Jesus went up to Jerusalem. Now there is in Jerusalem by the Sheep Gate a pool, which is called in Hebrew, Bethesda, having five porches. In these lay a great multitude of sick people, blind, lame, paralyzed, waiting for the moving of the water. For an angel went down at a certain time into the pool and stirred up the water; then whoever stepped in first, after the stirring of the water, was made well of whatever disease he had. Now a certain man was there who had an infirmity thirty-eight years. When Jesus saw him lying there, and knew that he already had been in that condition a long time, He said to him, "Do you want to be made well?"

The sick man answered Him, "Sir, I have no man to put me into the pool when the water is stirred up; but while I am coming, another steps down before me."

Jesus said to him, "Rise, take up your bed and walk." And immediately the man was made well, took up his bed, and walked. (John 5:1–9)

We know, on the opposite side or negative side, that demons or fallen angels can cause disease. There are many scriptures to back up this belief. *Luke 8:1–2* is just one example of this. It should not be strange or unusual to us that Holy angels can assist in healings and miracles.

Now it came to pass, afterward, that He went through every city and village, preaching and bringing the glad tidings of the kingdom of God. And the twelve were with Him, and certain women who had been healed of evil spirits and infirmities—Mary called Magdalene, out of whom had come seven demons, and Joanna the wife of Chuza, Herod's steward, and Susanna, and many others who provided for Him from their substance. (Luke 8:1–3)

As we understand and believe these events did happen, can happen, and will happen, the more we will experience them in our lives.

Jesus paid the price for redemption and healing; wholeness was a part of that redemption. Angels do play a vital role in delivering the promises of God to us and for us.

We operate by faith, and I believe, as we do this, we will see healings and bodies restored to the way God designed them to be. Diseases that medical science cannot fix, God can and will supernaturally fix them. And many times, angels will be involved in bringing those healings and new body parts to us.

The more we study, believe, and speak about angelic involvement in our lives, the more they will work and manifest themselves to us.

There are many testimonies of healings and miracles.

> Look at that! Look at that! The minister said, an angel has the man by the shoulders, and he's straightening the man up!

> The minister said to him, "All I can tell you is that there has been an angel standing right over here by the piano since the beginning of the service with a new heart for somebody."

> There's an angel holding her by her feet, straightening out her entire skeletal system right now!

> I was praying, and suddenly it felt like a hand went down on the inside of me, moved something, and took out that heart blockage.

All these quotes concerning healing by angels came from Mark Brazee book, *Angels: Heaven Helping Us*.

I believe that angels are real, and they are active in our lives daily. As we have already learned, angels are not moved by our needs, our circumstances, or our wants. They move and operate by the Word of God or by His direction. They work hand in hand with the Holy Spirit to bring about our confessions according to God's Word. The more we confess the Word, the more we believe angels exist, the more active they will be in our lives.

CHAPTER 9

Activating Angels

You and I have the authority to say certain things that will cause the angels to begin to operate in our lives with greater freedom and liberty. We say and do things that will hinder them in their work and ministry on our behalf. They have been sent to help us, and they desire to carry out God's plan for our life.

If we want more manifestations of angels in our lives, we need to be more aware of them, talk about them, and teach about them.

One minister was teaching and preaching on angels, and the Word of the Lord came forth saying, "You have created a habitation for angels."

We limit them in their ability to work when we don't use our faith and believe in them, when we don't teach and preach about them. They are here to assist us in our ministries and our daily lives.

Angels work where the Word of the Lord is taught and preached. Angels can work for people who believe in them.

1. We need angels helping us bring in the end-time harvest of souls.
2. We need angels protecting Christians.
3. We need angels to bring direction and instruction concerning our lives and the plan for our life.
4. We need angels to assist in healing, signs, miracles, and wonders.
5. We need angels operating in our finances, bringing in money and our supply.

6. We need angels helping us in our businesses to bring in customers, clients, and divine connections.
7. We need angels helping us in our ministries and our churches.
8. In other words, we need angels working and helping us in every aspect of our lives.
9. We should expect angel activity in our lives, because we need them and they are scriptural.

We have a covenant with God, and angels are just as much a part of that covenant as any other promise in the Bible.

It is a covenant promise that your angels will have charge over you and keep you healed, safe, and prosperous all the days of your life.

The main thing that hinders angels from working in our lives is the way we talk. Talking doubt and unbelief binds them and keeps them from working on our behalf.

Our negative confessions keep them from working on their assignments for us. They operate on and by God's Word.

> Bless the Lord, you His angels, who excel in strength, who do His word, Heeding the voice of His word. Bless the Lord, all you His hosts,
> You ministers of His, who do His pleasure. Bless the Lord, all His works, In all places of His dominion. (Psalm 103:20)

You can't ask your angels to do things that are contrary to the Bible and God's Word. Their only responsibility is to the Word of God.

> Do not let your mouth cause your flesh to sin, nor say before the messenger of God that it was an error. Why should God be angry at your excuse and destroy the work of your hands? For in the multitude of dreams and many words there is also vanity. But fear God. (Ecclesiastes 5:6)

When you talk contrary to His word, He is not able to protect you fully like He wants to.

Many Christians don't know or understand this realm and very little about angels themselves. That's why there are so many false teachings and beliefs concerning angels and their activity.

Just because we believe something is God's will for our lives does not necessarily mean it will just happen. We need to employ the help of our angels to bring it to pass.

In this study of angels, we have found out that God's Word outlines specific ways you can activate and deactivate your angels.

Many times, our angels are not working for us because we have not activated them in a proper biblical way. *Psalm 103:20* shows us the best way to activate angelic help in our lives.

> Bless the Lord, you His angels, Who excel
> in strength, who do His word, Heeding the voice
> of His word.

Did you notice that this scripture does not say that angels hearken to God's voice? (I am sure they do but this scripture tells us they specifically hearken to the voice of God's Word, and we give that Word voice when we speak it).

Angels get busy when we speak God's Word.

They go into action at the voice of God's Word.

God gave us His Word so we could speak it.

Every time you make a bold proclamation of God's Word, visualize angels taking off to do and hearken to that Word. Visualize the Word and angels working and bringing your needs, prayers, and supplications to pass.

Angels do not hearken to just any word but only to the Word of God.

They are waiting on my and your instruction to work for us and in our lives.

Because parents don't understand, sometimes they speak fear, doubt, and unbelief about and over their children that hinder the angels working and protecting them.

Many accidents and difficulties could be avoided if parents knew these things and used their faith. If they spoke according to the word of God.

> My people are destroyed for lack of knowl-
> edge. Because you have rejected knowledge, I also

will reject you from being priest for Me; Because
you have forgotten the law of your God, I also
will forget your children. (Hosea 4:6)

For indeed the gospel was preached to us as
well as to them; but the word which they heard
did not profit them, not being mixed with faith
in those who heard it. For we who have believed
do enter that rest, as He has said. (Hebrews 4:2)

For angels to work in your life, you must live right, act right,
and talk right.

Many times, because of previous or current sins, we hinder the
work of our angels. Many times, we open the door to the devil and
make it hard for our angels to accomplish God's will and His best for
our lives.

You can provoke your angel. To provoke means to grieve. Angels
are grieved when they cannot do what they are assigned to do. They
are here to help and provide for us. And when we provoke them by
our words and actions, we hinder their work here on earth.

Behold, I send an Angel before you to keep
you in the way and to bring you into the place
which I have prepared. Beware of Him and obey
His voice; do not provoke Him, for He will not
pardon your transgressions; for My name is in
Him. But if you indeed obey His voice and do all
that I speak, then I will be an enemy to your enemies and an adversary to your adversaries. For My
Angel will go before you and bring you in to the
Amorites and the Hittites and the Perizzites and
the Canaanites and the Hivites and the Jebusites;
and I will cut them off. (Exodus 23:20–23)

Psalm 17:3 tells us how we can provoke our angel by our words.
We need to learn to guard our mouth. We must learn to speak in line
with God's Word and His covenant.

You have tested my heart; You have visited
me in the night; You have tried me and have

found nothing; I have purposed that my mouth shall not transgress.

> Set a guard, O Lord, over my mouth; Keep watch over the door of my lips. (Psalm 141:3)

Jesus knew this, and He is our example!

> For I have not spoken on My own authority; but the Father who sent Me gave Me a command, what I should say and what I should speak. And I know that His command is everlasting life. Therefore, whatever I speak, just as the Father has told Me, so I speak. (John 12:49–50)

He was assured of the angelic ministry, and He understood their role. He had to put a voice to the Word, and so do we for the Word to work.

Angels will respond to what you say.

> Bless the Lord, you His angels, who excel in strength, who do His word, Heeding the voice of His word.
> Bless the Lord, all you His hosts, you minister of His, who do His pleasure. Bless the Lord, all His works, In all places of His dominion. Bless the Lord, O my soul! (Psalm 103:20–22)

> Hearkening unto the voice of his word. (vs 20)

The word *voice* just means "to call out, to call out the Word," *such as* the Lord is my strength; the Lord is my refuge; the Lord is my helper; He is my deliverer; he preserves me and my life. You have to say something, and it must be the Word of God. I am the head and not the tail. He delivers me from every evil. No evil shall befall me or my household. The Lord is my fortress.

The Word was spoken, so it could be written, so it could be spoken. Every Word written in the Bible was inspired by the Holy Spirit and given to man to be written so that we would have the Word to speak. That's the only way faith works—to speak it. You must give action to your faith, and speaking is how we do that. We speak the Word of God, and faith comes.

> And since we have the same spirit of faith, according to what is written, "I believed and therefore I spoke," we also believe and therefore speak. (2 Corinthians 4:13)

Psalm 91:11 says He charges His angels to keep you.

When we begin to speak God's Word by faith to the angels the same Word God has spoken, it activates the angels and their ministries.

God has already charged the angels but there is another charge that must be done, and that is done by you and me, speaking God's Word and sending our angels out to work on our behalf.

Angels are standing by waiting to hear us speak Words of faith out of our mouths.

> Also I say to you, whoever confesses Me before men, him the Son of Man also will confess before the angels of God. But he who denies Me before men will be denied before the angels of God.
>
> And anyone who speaks a word against the Son of Man, it will be forgiven him; but to him who blasphemes against the Holy Spirit, it will not be forgiven. (Luke 12:8–9)

When you start saying the Word of God, angels are released, dispatched, and activated to fulfill and bring to pass the Word of God in your life.

Example of a confession that will release angels to work on your behalf:

I am redeemed by the blood of the Lamb. I am delivered from every evil work. No evil shall come near me or my dwelling place. I am blessed coming and going. I am blessed in my business and in my ministry. Angels have been given charge over me and my household, and they are guarding and preserving me and my household. No weapon formed against me shall prosper, for I am a servant of God. I am the righteousness of God in Christ Jesus. I thank You, Father, that angels encamp all around me because I reverence you and am in covenant with you. I thank You in Jesus's name that my angels have charge over me.

Angels need words of faith to come out of your mouth based on the words of the covenant.

If you remember in Daniel 10:12, the angels said, "I came because of your words."

It was Daniel's words that brought the angel.

> Death and life are in the power of the
> tongue,
> And those who love it will eat its fruit.
> (Proverbs 18:21)

God made the world with words, and He designed everything to function and operate by words and by faith. It still operates that way today and it always will. God never changes!

> In the beginning God created the heavens and the earth. The earth was without form, and void; and darkness was on the face of the deep. And the Spirit of God was hovering over the face of the waters.
> Then God said, "Let there be light"; and there was light. And God saw the light, that it was good; and God divided the light from the darkness. (Genesis 1:1–4)

> For assuredly, I say to you, whoever says to this mountain, Be removed and be cast into the sea,' and does not doubt in his heart, but believes that those things he says will be done, he will have whatever he says. (Mark 11:23)

Before ending this chapter, we must also understand that there is another force that is listening to what we say—Satan and his fallen angels.

This group is full of death, destruction, and every evil work. They kill, steal, and destroy everything they meet that is not covered by our words of faith and by our covenant.

> The thief does not come except to steal, and
> to kill, and to destroy. I have come that they may
> have life, and that they may have it more abun-
> dantly. (John 10:10)

When you speak contrary words that do not line up with God's covenant, you give legal right to this group to disrupt your life.

> Lest Satan should take advantage of us; for we
> are not ignorant of his devices. (2 Corinthians 2:11)

> He winks his eye to devise perverse things;
> He pursues his lips and brings about evil.
> (Proverbs 16:30)

> If anyone among you thinks he is religious
> and does not bridle his tongue but deceives his own
> heart, this one's religion is useless. (James 1:26)

> The heart of the wise teaches his mouth,
> And adds learning to his lips. (Proverbs 16:23)

If we are to be covenant people, we must learn to talk like covenant people!

Kenneth Copeland said that angels are preprogrammed. What he meant was that angels have been programmed to activate, operate, and do the will of the Father when they hear His Word. What you say must be charged with the words they are programmed to.

God has charged His angels, His creation to respond to Him, and His Words alone. That probably changed after the fall of Satan and one-third of the angels listening to and hearkening to what Satan said. There are times when a computer must be reprogrammed to work as it was designed.

Angels are here for a purpose, and God designed them in a specific way, and that is the only way they will work for you.

I.   Important facts about angels and their purpose

    A.   Angels are agents of the government of God.
    B.   Their activities in the Bible are directly related to God's plans.

C. Nothing done by man controls angels.

1. The primary motivation of angels is to obey and serve God.
2. But man can do some things to activate them.

II. There are five biblical principles that activate angels. Our actions seem to influence their actions.

A. Obedience and submission to authority. When angels see us operating properly under authority, they are released to minister for us as the Holy Spirit wills.
B. Praise and worship

1. Music originally was ordained to worship our heavenly Father.
2. Satan perverted that.

a) Jesus—His temptation of Jesus in the wilderness was designed to get Jesus to worship him.
b) It failed because Jesus told him it was written that only God should be worshipped and served.
c) Job—Satan implied God could not be loved for Himself but only for what He does or gives people.
d) God allowed Satan to tempt Job because He knew Job's heart.
e) Jesus asked the multitude who followed Him after the feeding of the five thousand the same question.

(1) Jesus answered, "I tell you the truth, you are looking for me, not because you saw miraculous signs but because you ate the loaves and had your fill. Do not work for food that spoils, but for food that endures to eternal life, which the Son of Man will give you. On him God the Father has placed his seal of approval." (John 6:26)

      (2) Basically, Jesus was asking, "Are you following me because of who I am or what I can do for you?"

      (3) True worship comes out of love and reverence, not fear or a desire to be better off.

4. The song service in a church service is the procedure God designed for us to come into His presence.

    a) The first step is to approach God with thanksgiving.

      (1) Enter His gates with thanksgiving. (Psalm 100:4)

      (2) Thanksgiving is retelling what God has already done for you.

    b) The next step is to "enter His courts with praise" (same scripture), praising Him for who He is not for what He does.

3. *Second Chronicles 20:5–12* is a biblical example of how praise and worship activate the angels.

> Then Jehoshaphat stood in the assembly of Judah and Jerusalem, in the house of the Lord, before the new court, and said: "O Lord God of our fathers, are You not God in heaven, and do You not rule over all the kingdoms of the nations, and in Your hand is there not power and might, so that no one is able to withstand You? Are You not our God, who drove out the inhabitants of this land before Your people Israel, and gave it to the descendants of Abraham Your friend forever? And they dwell in it and have built You a sanctuary in it for Your name, saying, If disaster comes upon us—sword, judgment, pestilence, or famine—we will stand before this temple and in Your presence (for Your name is in this temple),

and cry out to You in our affliction, and You will hear and save.' And now, here are the people of Ammon, Moab, and Mount Seir—whom You would not let Israel invade when they came out of the land of Egypt, but they turned from them and did not destroy them—here they are, rewarding us by coming to throw us out of Your possession which You have given us to inherit. O our God, will You not judge them? For we have no power against this great multitude that is coming against us; nor do we know what to do, but our eyes are upon You." (2 Chronicles 20:5–12)

> a) The Israelites were surrounded.
> b) God told King Jehoshaphat to send the priests and singers before the army who sang and praised God that His mercy endures forever.
> c) *Verse 22* says that God set ambushments for the enemy. In the Bible, God consistently uses angels when He sets ambushments.

C. Sacrifice

> 1. Closely related to praise and worship
> 2. Abraham and David understood the principle of sacrifice.
>
> > a) Abraham: When he was willing to sacrifice his son, Isaac, an angel appeared to David.

And Gad came that day to David and said to him, "Go up, erect an altar to the Lord on the threshing floor of Araunah the Jebusite." So, David, according to the word of Gad, went up as the Lord commanded. Now Araunah looked and saw the king and his servants coming toward him. So Araunah went out and bowed before the king with his face to the ground.

Then Araunah said, "Why has my lord the king come to his servant?"

And David said, "To buy the threshing floor from you, to build an altar to the Lord, that the plague may be withdrawn from the people."

Now Araunah said to David, "Let my lord the king take and offer up whatever seems good to him. Look, here are oxen for burnt sacrifice, and threshing implements and the yokes of the oxen for wood. All these, O king, Araunah has given to the king." And Araunah said to the king, "May the Lord your God accept you." Then the king said to Araunah, "No, but I will surely buy it from you for a price; nor will I offer burnt offerings to the Lord my God with that which costs me nothing." So, David bought the threshing floor and the oxen for fifty shekels of silver. And David built there an altar to the Lord and offered burnt offerings and peace offerings. So, the Lord heeded the prayers for the land, and the plague was withdrawn from Israel. (2 Samuel 24:18–25)

And David said to God, "Was it not I who commanded the people to be numbered? I am the one who has sinned and done evil; indeed, but these sheep, what have they done? Let Your hand, I pray, O Lord my God, be against me and my father's house, but not against Your people that they should be plagued."

Therefore, the angel of the Lord commanded Gad to say to David that David should go and erect an altar to the Lord on the threshing floor of Ornan the Jebusite. So, David went up at the word of Gad, which he had spoken in the name of the Lord. Now Ornan turned and saw the angel; and his four sons who were with him hid themselves, but Ornan continued threshing wheat. So, David came to Ornan, and Ornan looked and saw David. And he went out from the threshing floor and bowed before David with his face to the ground. Then David said to Ornan, "Grant me the place of this threshing floor, that

I may build an altar on it to the Lord. You shall grant it to me at the full price, that the plague may be withdrawn from the people."

But Ornan said to David, "Take it to yourself, and let my lord the king does what is good in his eyes. Look, I also give you the oxen for burnt offerings, the threshing implements for wood, and the wheat for the grain offering; I give it all."

Then King David said to Ornan, "No, but I will surely buy it for the full price, for I will not take what is yours for the Lord, nor offer burnt offerings with that which costs me nothing." So, David gave Ornan six hundred shekels of gold by weight for the place. And David built there an altar to the Lord, and offered burnt offerings and peace offerings, and called on the Lord; and He answered him from heaven by fire on the altar of burnt offering. So, the Lord commanded the angel, and he returned his sword to its sheath.

At that time, when David saw that the Lord had answered him on the threshing floor of Ornan the Jebusite, he sacrificed there. For the tabernacle of the Lord and the altar of the burnt offering, which Moses had made in the wilderness, were at that time at the high place in Gibeon. But David could not go before it to inquire of God, for he was afraid of the sword of the angel of the Lord. (1 Chronicles 21:17–30)

Second Chronicles 3:1 states that there was offered sacrifice to God on the threshing floor of Ornan to stop the death angel.

Now Solomon began to build the house of the Lord at Jerusalem on Mount Moriah, where the Lord had appeared to his father David, at the place that David had prepared on the threshing floor of Ornan the Jebusite.

3. Why does God require sacrifice?

    a) In the Old Testament, the only way to approach God's holiness was through the substitutionary death of a living creature.

    b) Blood is proof of such death because life is in the blood—animal sacrifice, substitution of Jesus's sacrifice to come.

Only be sure that you do not eat the blood,
for the blood is the life; you may not eat the life
with the meat. (Deuteronomy 12:23)

    c) David refused to receive the threshing floor of Ornan as a gift but paid full price for it because he knew it was not a real offering unless it cost him something.

    d) We would prefer to praise God when everything is going well and grumble and complain when it is not.

        (1) That attitude will not activate the angels.

        (2) Sacrificial worship, despite the circumstances, provides the legal right for the angels to come and help us.

D. Praying the Word

1. The primary way to renew our mind so that any thoughts dropped in by evil spirits cannot find a lodging place is to meditate on the word.

2. Something special happens in the angelic realm when Christians speak God's Word during bad circumstances.

    a) When we pray the Word, it allows us to get in agreement with God.

    b) It releases the angels to work alongside of us.

    c) When we pray the problem, we are trying to get God in agreement with us. Instead, we should be praying God's promises.

    d) Problems do not activate angels, God's word does.

3. Promises from God's Word brings provision, including help of angels.
4. God does not need to hear the problem; He already knows it.

   a) He wants to hear the promise that will fix the problem.
   b) He wants to hear us praise Him in advance for that promise.
   c) He honors prayer that costs us something.

5. Prayer by the church brought the angel to Peter in prison. Prayer brought the angel to shut the lions' mouths for Daniel.

E. Giving in obedience

1. Giving to God's work, God's people—poor and needy—activates angels.
2. Something about money and its use by us touch the angelic realm.
3. Sacrificial giving activates angels as much as sacrificial praise.
4. When Satan became the "god of this world," he became authority over the finances of the world, and everything that belongs to the world system.

   a) When Jesus died on the cross, the authority over finances once again became God's.
   b) Because God has given us responsibility to reach the world, He has given us the authority to get the job done.
   c) We should be taking authority over gold and silver through biblical principles.
   d) More than anything else our stewardship in finances demonstrates whether we have come under God's authority.
   e) The angels are aware of how we handle money.

5. Three important steps to activating angels in the financial realm

a) Claim what you need.
b) Tell the devil to take his hands off the money and/or resources.
c) Tell the ministering angels to go and bring you what you need.
d) The angels are waiting for you to give directions according to the Word of God and by the direction of the Holy Spirit.

God is no respecter of persons, and His angels are ready to bring your supply when you speak His Word.

Angels are mighty and excel in strength, according to *Psalm 3:20*. Your prayers open the door for angels to work and get busy on your behalf. Being a person of prayer and walking in the supernatural go hand in hand.

Growing up, I heard preachers tell us to pray through to God. God lives in us through the Holy Spirit. The only praying through that we need to do is pray through all the hell that Satan has thrown our way. To pray through all the demonic influence that has come against us in our minds and our lives, it will lead to a prosperous, healthy and victorious life.

Many times, we pray and tell God how to help us, and instead we should pray and ask for help and let God tell us how He wants to help and let Him tell us the plan for deliverance in our situation. Then we can come in agreement and activate our angels according to His Word and instruction.

In the Old Testament, they prayed down the victory.

In the New Testament, we already have the victory through Jesus's death, burial, and resurrection. We just need to walk in it, speak it, and activate our angels according to the Word and then receive it.

CHAPTER 10

Can a Christian Be Demon Possessed?

I. There are two different meanings in the New Testament describing a person who has a demon:

A. One who is demonized

1. The demon cannot be successfully resisted by the person and indwells the person.
2. Indwelling a person is not easy; it must be a willing host.
3. It may leave the person temporarily and then return.
4. Once a demon has indwelt a person, that person is susceptible to a renewed invasion if they are not in a proper spiritual condition: They should be praying regularly, reading their Bible regularly, fellowshipping with other believers regularly and/or attending a Bible believing church.

B. One under the influence of a demon

II. There are three levels of attack from a demon.

A. Oppression—evil thoughts that encourage carnal sins and affect the mind and emotions
B. Obsession—continual attack in a certain area (example: lust, pornography).

C. Possession—to own; having indwelling spirit that runs a person's life; indwelt in human spirit.

III. When a person becomes born-again, the Holy Spirit comes to live in the human spirit.

    A. Christians cannot be possessed by a demon because the Holy Spirit owns us. Christians cannot be owned by an evil spirit and The Holy Spirit at the same time.

    B. The body and soul of a Christian can be oppressed, obsessed, and influenced by demons.

Questions concerning demons:

1. Should a Christian fear demons?

No! Throughout Scripture, we are told that we, as believers, have dominion and power over the evil forces that come against us.

The question comes up sometimes: Can Christians be demonized?

Demons come to torment, destroy, and cause chaos in people's lives. Demons can and will work freely in even Christians' lives unless we take authority over them.

Demons cannot possess a born-again Christian, but they can influence, cause chaos, and even destroy one's life if they are allowed to continue working in the person's life.

> And Jesus came and spoke to them, saying, "All authority has been given to Me in heaven and on earth. Go therefore and make disciples of all the nations, baptizing them in the name of the Father and of the Son and of the Holy Spirit, teaching them to observe all things that I have commanded you; and lo, I am with you always, even to the end of the age." Amen. (Matthew 28:18–20)

> Then the seventy returned with joy, saying, "Lord, even the demons are subject to us in Your name."

> And He said to them, "I saw Satan fall like lightning from heaven. Behold, I give you the authority to trample on serpents and scorpions, and over all the power of the enemy, and nothing shall by any means hurt you. Nevertheless do not rejoice in this, that the spirits are subject to you, but rather rejoice because your names are written in heaven." (Luke 10:17–20)

2. When a demon is cast out, is there danger or possibility of it just randomly harassing or attacking an innocent bystander?

No! The person who is exorcising a demon and sets the possessed person free can tell the demon what it can and cannot do.

Example: In Matthew 8, Jesus cast out the demons that whinnied and pleaded with Jesus.

> Now a good way off from them there was a herd of many swine feeding. So the demons begged Him, saying, "If You cast us out, permit us to go away into the herd of swine."
>
> And He said to them, "Go." So, when they had come out, they went into the herd of swine. And suddenly the whole herd of swine ran violently down the steep place into the sea and perished in the water. (Matthew 8:30–32)

3. Is there a connection between demons, drug, and alcohol abuse?

I believe most addictions are influenced by demons; that's the reason there is no medical cure for most addictions. The only medicine that will work and last is to first be set free spiritually from the demonic influence. A person that is being oppressed or depressed should immerse themselves in the Word of God to build their faith and strengthen their shield of faith. Once a person who is possessed is set free, they should immerse themselves in the Word and continually be around people who are of faith and can help them when temptation comes.

Not only the addicted but the people who are dealers of these addictions are also being influenced by the demonic powers of darkness.

Demons can gain ground in a person through an unprotected thought life.

They can gain ground through our eyes and ears also. It is important we live a Spirit-filled life and maintain it through the Word.

4.   Can evil spirits live in material buildings?

Yes! Evil spirits can live and possess anything or any place that welcomes it in—any place that it can assume authority and not have to worry about being hindered from its evil deeds (such as a bar, nightclub, or a home that invites these spirits in).

Fallen angels feel as if they need to communicate, and they will make their home anywhere they are not resisted. An evil spirit usually won't dwell in an empty building, but they can possess and manifest themselves in buildings humans are in.

5.   Who can cast out demons?

Jesus commissioned or commanded His disciples to cast out demons.

> And these signs will follow those who believe: In My name they will cast out demons; they will speak with new tongues; they will take up serpents; and if they drink anything deadly, it will by no means hurt them; they will lay hands on the sick, and they will recover. (Mark 16:17–18)

> Then He called His twelve disciples together and gave them *power and authority over all demons*, and to cure diseases. [2] He sent them to preach the kingdom of God and to heal the sick. (Luke 9:1–2)

We find in *Luke 17*, when the seventy returned, they were astonished that the devils and demons were subject to them and their commands by just pronouncing the name of Jesus.

The Word tells us in *Mark 16:15–17* that Jesus specifically said that those who believe would cast out devils, not just pastors, bishops or church leaders but believers! A believer is someone who has accepted Jesus as their personal Lord and Savior.

> And He said to them, "Go into all the world and preach the gospel to every creature. He who believes and is baptized will be saved; but he who does not believe will be condemned. And these signs will follow those who believe: *In My name they will cast out demons*; they will speak with new tongues; they will take up serpents; and if they drink anything deadly, it will by no means hurt them; they will lay hands on the sick, and they will recover." (Mark 16:15–18)

There are many ways to get rid of demons that are working in our lives. We get rid of demons the same way Jesus did. We remove them by using the Word against them.

Here are a few things that help invite demons into our lives: anger, sin, dirty talk, pornography, Homosexuality, and any other sin that goes unattended and remains in our lives.

Demons influence people today by bringing false doctrines and teachings into their lives.

We must understand, demons are no match for a spirit-filled believer. We have been given complete authority and power over Satan and his demons.

The Holy Spirit that lives inside you and me is the same Holy Spirit that raised Jesus from the dead. God's power is never failing. It will always produce power and authority in our lives as we grow and allow the Holy Spirit to have more control in our lives.

6. Do demons or demon spirits have specific names?

There were several names used in the Bible to identify demons.

> Spirit of infirmity
> And behold, there was a woman who had *a spirit of infirmity* eighteen years and was bent over and could in no way raise herself up. But

when Jesus saw her, He called her to Him and said to her, "Woman, you are loosed from your infirmity." And He laid His hands on her, and immediately she was made straight, and glorified God. (Luke 13:11–13)

Dumb and deaf spirit

When Jesus saw that the people came running together, He rebuked the unclean spirit, saying to it, *"Deaf and dumb spirit,* I command you, come out of him and enter him no more!" Then the spirit cried out, convulsed him greatly, and came out of him. And he became as one dead, so that many said, "He is dead." But Jesus took him by the hand and lifted him up, and he arose.

And when He had come into the house, His disciples asked Him privately, "Why could we not cast it out?"

So He said to them, "This kind can come out by nothing but prayer and fasting." (Mark 9:25–29)

A dragon

And war broke out in heaven: Michael and his angels fought with *the dragon*; and the dragon and his angels fought, but they did not prevail, nor was a place found for them in heaven any longer. So the great dragon was cast out, that serpent of old, called the Devil and Satan, who deceives the whole world; he was cast to the earth, and his angels were cast out with him.

Then I heard a loud voice saying in heaven, "Now salvation, and strength, and the kingdom of our God, and the power of His Christ have come, for the accuser of our brethren, who accused them before our God day and night, has been cast down. And they overcame him by the blood of the Lamb and by the word of their testimony, and they did not love their lives to the death. Therefore rejoice, O heavens, and you who dwell in them! Woe to the inhabitants of the earth and the sea! For the devil has come down to you, having great wrath, because he knows that he has a short time." (Revelation 12:7–12)

Jealous spirit

If *the spirit of jealousy* comes upon him and he becomes jealous of his wife, who has defiled herself; or if the spirit of jealousy comes upon him and he becomes jealous of his wife, although she has not defiled herself—then the man shall bring his wife to the priest. (Numbers 5:14–15)

This is *the law of jealousy,* when a wife, while under her husband's authority, goes astray and defiles herself, or when the spirit of jealousy comes upon a man, and he becomes jealous of his wife; then he shall stand the woman before the LORD, and the priest shall execute all this law upon her. Then the man shall be free from iniquity, but that woman shall bear her guilt. (Numbers 5:29–31)

Seducing spirit

Now the Spirit expressly says that in latter times some will depart from the faith, giving heed to *deceiving spirits and doctrines of demons,* speaking lies in hypocrisy, having their own conscience seared with a hot iron, forbidding to marry, and commanding to abstain from foods which God created to be received with thanksgiving by those who believe and know the truth. For every creature of God is good, and nothing is to be refused if it is received with thanksgiving; for it is sanctified by the word of God and prayer. (1 Timothy 4:1–5)

A lying spirit

The LORD said to him, 'In what way?' So, he said, 'I will go out and be *a lying spirit in* the mouth of all his prophets.' And the LORD said, you shall persuade him, and also prevail. Go out and do so.' [23] Therefore look! The LORD has put *a lying spirit* in the mouth of all these prophets of yours, and the LORD has declared disaster against you." (1 Kings 22:22–23)

Then a spirit came forward and stood before the LORD, and said, 'I will persuade him.' The LORD said to him, 'In what way?' So he said, 'I will go out and *be a lying spirit* in the mouth of all his prophets.' And the LORD said, 'You shall persuade him and also prevail; go out and do so.' Therefore look! The LORD has put a lying spirit in the mouth of these prophets of yours, and the LORD has declared disaster against you." (2 Chronicles 18:20–22)

Unclean spirit (used over twenty times)
And as he was still coming, the demon threw him down and convulsed him. Then Jesus rebuked *the unclean spirit,* healed the child, and gave him back to his father. (Luke 9:42)

When *an unclean spirit* goes out of a man, he goes through dry places, seeking rest, and finds none. Then he says, 'I will return to my house from which I came.' And when he comes, he finds it empty, swept, and put in order. Then he goes and takes with him seven other spirits more wicked than himself, and they enter and dwell there; and the last state of that man is worse than the first. So shall it also be with this wicked generation." (Matthew 12:43–45)

Now there was a man in their synagogue with an *unclean spirit.* And he cried out, saying, "Let us alone! What have we to do with You, Jesus of Nazareth? Did You come to destroy us? I know who You are—the Holy One of God!"
But Jesus rebuked him, saying, "Be quiet, and come out of him!" And when the *unclean spirit* had convulsed him and cried out with a

loud voice, he came out of him. Then they were all amazed, so that they questioned among themselves, saying, "What is this? What new doctrine is this? For with authority, He commands *even the unclean spirits,* and they obey Him." And immediately His fame spread throughout all the region around Galilee. (Mark 1:23–28)

Blind spirit
Then one was brought to Him who was demon-possessed, blind and mute; and He healed him, so that the blind and mute man both spoke and saw. And all the multitudes were amazed and said, "Could this be the Son of David?"

Now when the Pharisees heard it, they said, "This fellow does not cast out demons except by Beelzebub, the ruler of the demons." (Matthew 12:22–24)

Angel of light
And no wonder! For Satan himself transforms himself into *an angel of light.* Therefore it is no great thing if his ministers also transform themselves into ministers of righteousness, whose end will be according to their works. (2 Corinthians 11:14–15)

A lion
Be sober, be vigilant; because your adversary the devil walks about like *a roaring lion,* seeking whom he may devour. Resist him, steadfast in the faith, knowing that the same sufferings are experienced by your brotherhood in the world. (1 Peter 5:8–9)

Binding spirit
Now the Spirit expressly says that in latter times some will depart from the faith, giving heed to deceiving spirits and doctrines of demons, speaking lies in hypocrisy, having their own

conscience seared with a hot iron, forbidding to marry, and commanding to abstain from foods which God created to be received with thanksgiving by those who believe and know the truth. For every creature of God is good, and nothing is to be refused if it is received with thanksgiving; for it is sanctified by the word of God and prayer. (1 Timothy 4:1–5)

A foul spirit

When Jesus saw that the people came running together, He rebuked the unclean spirit, saying to it, "Deaf and dumb spirit, I command you, come out of him and enter him no more!" Then the spirit cried out, convulsed him greatly, and came out of him. And he became as one dead, so that many said, "He is dead." But Jesus took him by the hand and lifted him up, and he arose.

And when He had come into the house, His disciples asked Him privately, "Why could we not cast it out?"

So He said to them, "This kind can come out by nothing but prayer and fasting." (Mark 9:25–29)

After these things I saw another angel coming down from heaven, having great authority, and the earth was illuminated with his glory. And he cried mightily with a loud voice, saying, "Babylon the great is fallen, is fallen, and has become a dwelling place of demons, a prison *for every foul spirit,* and a cage for every unclean and hated bird! For all the nations have drunk of the wine of the wrath of her fornication, the kings of the earth have committed fornication with her, and the merchants of the earth have become rich through the abundance of her luxury. (Revelation 18:1–3)

The main thing to remember is Jesus gave you authority over *all* spirits. It doesn't matter what they call themselves.

And when He had called His twelve disciples to Him, *He gave them power over unclean spirits, to cast them out, and to heal all kinds of sickness and all kinds of disease.* Now the names of the twelve apostles are these: first, Simon, who is called Peter, and Andrew his brother; James the son of Zebedee, and John his brother; Philip and Bartholomew; Thomas and Matthew the tax collector; James the son of Alphaeus, and Lebbaeus, whose surname was Thaddaeus; Simon the Cananite, and Judas Iscariot, who also betrayed Him. Sending Out the Twelve

These twelve Jesus sent out and commanded them, saying: "Do not go into the way of the Gentiles, and do not enter a city of the Samaritans. But go rather to the lost sheep of the house of Israel. And as you go, preach, saying, the kingdom of heaven is at hand.' Heal the sick, cleanse the lepers, raise the dead, cast out demons. Freely you have received, freely give. Provide neither gold nor silver nor copper in your money belts, nor bag for your journey, nor two tunics, nor sandals, nor staffs; for a worker is worthy of his food. (Matthew 10:1–10)

Then He called His twelve disciples together and *gave them power and authority over all demons, and to cure diseases.* He sent them to preach the kingdom of God and to heal the sick. And He said to them, "Take nothing for the journey, neither staffs nor bag nor bread nor money; and do not have two tunics apiece.

"Whatever house you enter, stay there, and from there depart. And whoever will not receive you, when you go out of that city, shake off the very dust from your feet as a testimony against them."

> So they departed and went through the towns, preaching the gospel and healing every-where. (Luke 9:1–6)

7.   Why should we believe we have authority over angels, demons and devils?

We find in the Old Testament that Jacob prevailed and wrestled with an angel (*Genesis 32:24–29*).

> Then Jacob was left alone; and a Man wres-tled with him until the breaking of day. Now when He saw that He did not prevail against him, He touched the socket of his hip; and the socket of Jacob's hip was out of joint as He wres-tled with him. And He said, "Let Me go, for the day breaks."
> But he said, "I will not let You go unless You bless me!"
> So He said to him, "What is your name?"
> He said, "Jacob."
> And He said, "Your name shall no longer be called Jacob, but Israel; for you have struggled with God and with men, and have prevailed."
> Then Jacob asked, saying, "Tell me Your name, I pray."
> And He said, "Why is it that you ask about My name?" And He blessed him there.
> So Jacob called the name of the place Peniel: "For I have seen God face to face, and my life is preserved." Just as he crossed over Penuel the sun rose on him, and he limped on his hip. Therefore to this day the children of Israel do not eat the muscle that shrank, which is on the hip socket, because He touched the socket of Jacob's hip in the muscle that shrank. (Genesis 32:24–32)

If he had authority over demons under the old covenant, how much more do we have under the new, revised, and better covenant (*Hebrews 8:6*)?

For if that first covenant had been fault-less, then no place would have been sought for a second. Because finding fault with them, He says: "Behold, the days are coming, says the LORD, when I will make a new covenant with the house of Israel and with the house of Judah—not according to the covenant that I made with their fathers in the day when I took them by the hand to lead them out of the land of Egypt; because they did not continue in My covenant, and I disregarded them, says the LORD. For this is the covenant that I will make with the house of Israel after those days, says the LORD: I will put My laws in their mind and write them on their hearts; and I will be their God, and they shall be My people. None of them shall teach his neighbor, and none his brother, saying, 'Know the LORD,' for all shall know Me, from the least of them to the greatest of them. For I will be merciful to their unrigh-teousness, and their sins and their lawless deeds I will remember no more."

In that He says, "A new covenant," He has made the first obsolete. Now what is becoming obsolete and growing old is ready to vanish away. (Hebrews 8:7–13)

We find a scripture in the Old Testament that is confusing to many believers. In *Genesis 1:26* it says, "Let us (Elohim) make man in our image… Then God said, 'Let Us make man in Our image, according to Our likeness; let them have dominion over the fish of the sea, over the birds of the air, and over the cattle, over all the earth and over every creeping thing that creeps on the earth.' So God cre-ated man in His own image; in the image of God He created him; male and female He created them. Then God blessed them, and God said to them, 'Be fruitful and multiply; fill the earth and subdue it; have dominion over the fish of the sea, over the birds of the air, and over every living thing that moves on the earth'" (Genesis 1:26–28).

We find in Psalm 8:5 that God made man a little lower than the angels. The word "angels" is not in the original language or manuscript. In reality, Psalm 8:5 should read, "Thou hast made him (man) a littler lower than God."

> What is man that You are mindful of him,
> And the son of man that You visit him?
> For You have made him a little lower than the angels,
> And You have crowned him with glory and honor.
> You have made him to have dominion over the works of Your hands; You have put all things under his feet, All sheep and oxen—Even the beasts of the field, The birds of the air,
> And the fish of the sea That pass through the paths of the seas. (Psalm 8:4–8)

We were created to be sons and daughters of God, and angels were created to be servants.

In *Romans 8:17*, we find we are heirs and joint heirs of God.

> The Spirit Himself bears witness with our spirit that we are children of God, and if children, then heirs—heirs of God and joint heirs with Christ, if indeed we suffer with Him, that we may also be glorified together. (Romans 8:16–17)

When we became born-again, we became new creatures with new authority and power that would enable us to tread on serpents and cast out demons and devils.

The Bible tells us that we will someday judge angels. I believe this means we will someday judge the fallen angel (*1 Corinthians 6:3*).

> Dare any of you, having a matter against another, go to law before the unrighteous, and not before the saints? Do you not know that the saints will judge the world? And if the world will be judged by you, are you unworthy to judge the smallest matters? *Do you not know that we shall judge angels?* How much more, things that

pertain to this life? If then you have judgments concerning things pertaining to this life, do you appoint those who are least esteemed by the church to judge? I say this to your shame. Is it so, that there is not a wise man among you, not even one, who will be able to judge between his brethren? But brother goes to law against brother, and that before unbelievers! (1 Corinthians 6:1–6)

Many times, we place way too much emphasis on demons and their power, and many times Christians believe they don't exist, and so we can have two extremes.

Demons are real! There are personal demons, and then there are territorial demons. Most people and Christians will deal with personal demons more so than territorial ones. In the Bible, the personal demons are called unclean spirits, and the territorial demons are assigned to specific areas, homes, churches, workplace, schools, government, the media, such as TV, internet, etc.

Both kinds of demons are defeated by allowing Jesus, the Word, and the Holy Spirit to work in our lives.

CHAPTER 11

The Truth about Angels

I. We should never accept anything supernatural without testing its source.

   A. Test everything. Hold on to the good. (1 Thessalonians 5:21)

   B. Do not believe every spirit, but test the spirits to see whether they are from God… (1 John 4:1)

There are many spirits but none as powerful as the Holy Spirit.

II. How to test angels:

   A. See if the visit matches those of the Bible.
   B. Listen to see if the angel's words line up with the Bible.
   C. Check to see if the purpose, which their visit achieves, is biblical.

III. You can know an angel is false if he…

   A. Says he is the spirit of a dead friend or ancestor.
   B. Draws attention to self and away from Jesus and God. (Good angels never brings attention to self.)
   C. Brings revelation that cannot be found in the Bible.
   D. Says all religions are of God, and the hereafter is a good place for everyone.

E. Entertains and socializes after his "assignment" is over. (Good angels appear, give their message, or help in danger and vanish.)
F. Uses spectacular lights, weird sounds, or odd odors to get your attention.
G. Flatters you and builds up your pride, telling you how spiritual you are.
H. Leaves you feeling anxious, fearful, confused. (Good angels bring peace.)
I. Tries to force you to do something against your inner witness.
J. Results of visit is harmful to you or those around you.
K. Tells you that you can talk to him anytime, call him in some way, or that he lives within you. (Good angels never become a part of a person.)

You cannot test angels if you do not know the Bible.
There are four specific things angels do for us.

1. They protect us. We get our belief in guardian angels from Matthew 12:7–10 and Psalm 91:11.
2. They assist us in our ministry and assignments that God gives us.

Angels are busy around us, making arrangement for us to meet divine appointments and situations for us. We are to do all we can in the natural and depend on them to carry out the supernatural.

3. Angels will escort us to heaven when we die.

The best illustration of this is the story of Lazarus and the rich man in Luke 16:22.

4. Angels execute God's judgments.

We find our first and best example in the Old Testament in Genesis 19:13 with the story of Sodom and Gomorrah.
In the book of Revelation, we find where angels bring judgment on the earth.
In the very end, when the lost are judged, angels will have the assignment of casting them into the lake of fire with Satan and all his demons.

CHAPTER 12

Bible Stories Concerning Angels and Their Benefit

1. In *2 Kings 6*, we find that God sent angels to rescue and assist the prophet Elisha.

The king of Syria came against Israel, setting a trap for them. But God empowered Elisha to supernaturally know where the trap had been set and warned the king, saying, "Don't go that way, it's a trap." We find that the Israelites went a separate way, and the Syrian army set another trap. Again, the prophet of God had inside information and told the king of Israel, "Don't go that direction, there's a trap set for you." This happened over and over until the king of Syria thought there had to be a spy in the camp.

Second King 6:15 states that Elisha's servant wanted to know what in the world they were going to do when he saw the camp was surrounded by the Syrian Army. "Fear Not," Elisha said. Elisha got his advice from God. He told the servant to fear not for those who are with us are more than those who are with them. In other words, they had supernatural backup. We find that Elisha asked God to open the servants' eyes and let him see into the spirit realm.

**(Whether you can see it or not, there will always be angelic help, supernatural help around you, protecting you, advising you, and ministering to you).*

2. Another Old Testament example is the story of a sound in the mulberry trees!

Chronicles 14:9–10, 12 is a story of King David who drove the Philistines off God's territory.

David basically inquired of God and asked what they were going to do. God answered and said, "Go, and I will deliver them into your hands." David obeyed God, and He delivered them from their enemies. David destroyed all their gods and burned them. We find that the Philistines came back for a second go-round with King David. David inquired of God again, and God told David, "Don't go up after them." This was different from the first instructions given. **This is a great Bible example of how important it is to be led by the Spirit of God, "then and now."

One of the most important lessons a believer can learn is how to be led by the Spirit of God. Many times, we find ourselves in the same situation as before, and we just automatically do what we did the first time because it worked that time. Getting in a rut of doing the same thing over and over will eventually get you in trouble. King David didn't just charge into battle like the first time, he asked God what to do. We should all get in the habit of continually asking God, "What do you want me to do in this situation?" "What will work this time?" "What is right for this time and situation?"

King David had the Spirit of God upon him, and with him, we have a better covenant and have the Holy Spirit always living inside us.

When David inquired of God in *1 Chronicles 14:14*, God told him, "Go not up after them, turn away from them, and come upon them over against the mulberry trees."

God told David to turn and fake them out.

In 1 Chronicles 14:15–17:

Verse 15, "It shall be, when thou shalt hear a sound of going in the tops of the mulberry trees…"

Verse 15 from the Amplified Bible: "When you hear a sound of marching in the top of the mulberry trees…"

Verse 15 from the Message Bible: "When you hear the sound of shuffling feet in the top of the balsams…"

Verse 15 from the Basic English Bible: "And at the sound of footsteps in the top of the trees, go out to fight, for God has gone out before you to overcome the Philistine army."

Here is the best translation of this verse from the original Aramaic Bible: "When thou shall hear the sound of the angels coming to thy assistance, then go out to do battle, for an angel is sent from the presence of the God that He may render thy way prosperous."

When David and his army heard the shuffling in the mulberry trees, that was their signal or sign to do as God had said.

God had sent His angels to confuse and deliver the Philistines and make David's way prosperous.

New Testament examples:

1. Angels announced Jesus's birth, His ministry, and His resurrection.

   And when Jesus returns in the clouds, He will be surrounded by His angelic force.
   Luke 2:9–14 states that angels appeared to the shepherds that were watching over their flocks.

2. When Jesus was in the wilderness being tempted by the devil.
   Matthew 4 states that after Jesus was tempted and fasted for forty days and forty nights, angels ministered to Him.
3. Angels were present when Jesus was raised from the dead.

   Very early in the morning, on the first day of the week, they came to the tomb when the sun had risen. And they said among themselves, "Who will roll away the stone from the door of the tomb for us?" But when they looked up, they saw that the stone had been rolled away—for it was very large. And entering the tomb, they saw a young man clothed in a long white robe sitting on the right side; and they were alarmed. But he said to them, "Do not be alarmed. You seek Jesus of Nazareth, who was crucified. He is risen! He is not here. See the place where they laid Him. (Mark 16:2–6)

4.   In Acts 12, we see a jailbreak that angels played a huge part in.

Peter was going to be killed and was being held in a maximum-security jail of that time. As soon as the church saw the situation, they began to pray. The Bible says, "They went to instant and earnest prayer" (Acts 12:5). The church was probably grieving the death of James. Herod had already killed him, and Peter was to be next. While the church was praying, an angel showed up at the prison. It was night, and Peter was sleeping between soldiers. Peter was in what seemed like a desperate and hopeless situation. God was and is greater than what Peter was facing, and He is greater than what you are facing.

The doors were locked. The guards were there to keep him from escaping. Peter was on the cold damp floor, locked in chains. It appeared to be a no-win situation, but Peter slept! Do you think Peter may have turned it all over to God and was resting in His promise that God would protect and deliver him just as He did Daniel so many times? He will do the same for you and me. The Bible says, "But suddenly, there was a bright light shined into the prison. Prayers were being answered, and help had arrived." Peter was so at rest; he didn't even see the light. He was so sound asleep; the angel had to nudge him to wake him up.

Then the instructions came from the angel!

    a.   Get up.
    b.   Get your coat on.
    c.   Get your shoes on.
    d.   Let's get out of here.

None of the soldiers heard or saw anything; they slept right through all the commotion.

The chains fell off, and Peter walked right out the doors that opened supernaturally.

The angel disappeared, and Peter went to where the church was still in prayer. They were in such earnest praying; they didn't hear him when he was knocking on the door. They were determined to pray until Peter was delivered, and their prayers brought an angel on the scene.

Corporate prayer or united prayer is a wonderful way to get the job done when it seems nothing else is working. We need to have the same revelation the early church had and be more earnest in our praying.

Review:

1. If God can use an angel to strengthen Daniel during prayer (*Daniel 9:21*), He can use an angel to help us today.
2. If God can send an angel to reveal Zechariah the meaning of a vision, He was showing the prophet (*Zechariah 1:9*), He can use an angel to communicate to you and me today.
3. If God can send the angel Gabriel to reveal the future to Daniel (*Daniel 8:16*), He can use an angel to explain ideas and situations to you and me today.
4. If God can use an angel to instruct Philip the evangelist what to do (*Acts 8:26*), He can use an angel to give us direction today.
5. If God can use an angel to quicken Daniel's mind and give him the skill to understand the things of God (*Daniel 9:22*), He can use an angel to give us insight and to help us understand the Word today.
6. If God can give the entire book of Revelation to John by an angel (*Revelation 1:1*), He can use an angel to tell us about our future.
7. If God can use an angel to explain a vision to Daniel (*Daniel 8:16*), He can use an angel to clarify things for us today.

CHAPTER 13

Topical Index for "Angel"

1. ANGEL (a spirit), ANGEL, (Holy Trinity), ANGEL OF THE CHURCHES
2. ABADDON: The angel of the bottomless pit (Revelation 9:11)
3. ABRAHAM: Angels appear to (Genesis 18:1–16; 22:11, 15; 24:7)
4. APOLLYON: Angel of the bottomless pit (Revelation 9:11)
5. ARCHANGEL: See ANGEL
6. ASSYRIA: Army of, destroyed by the angel of the Lord (Isaiah 37:36)
7. CAPTAIN: Angel of the Lord, called (Joshua 5:14; 2 Chronicles 13:12)
8. EL-BETH-EL: Name of the altar erected by Jacob where he had the vision of angels (Genesis 35:7)
9. GIDEON: Call of, by an angel (Judges 6:11,14)
10. GIDEON: Angel attests the call to, by miracle (Judges 6:21–24)
11. HOMAGE: By the angel seen by John in his vision (Revelation 19:10; 22:8, 9)
12. JACOB: Meets angels of God on the journey and calls the place "Mahanaim" (Genesis 32:1, 2)
13. JACOB: Dreads to meet Esau; sends him presents; wrestles with an angel (Genesis 32)
14. LEGION: Of angels (Matthew 26:53)

15. MAHANAIM: The place where Jacob had the vision of angels (Genesis 32:2)
16. MAN: LITTLE LOWER THAN THE ANGELS (Job 4:18–21; Psalms 8:5; Hebrews 2:7, 8)
17. PETER: Imprisoned and delivered by an angel (Acts 12:3–19)
18. PROPHETS: Inspired by angels (Zechariah 1:9, 13, 14, 19; Acts 7:53; Galatians 3:19; Hebrews 2:2)
19. SATAN: The angel of the bottomless pit (Revelation 9:11)
20. SHEPHERD: Angels appeared to (Luke 2:8–20)
21. SPIRIT: See ANGELS
22. WORSHIP: Of angels, forbidden (Revelation 19:10; 22:8, 9)
23. Called ANGEL OF HIS PRESENCE (Isaiah 63:9)
24. Men called angels (2 Samuel 19:27)
25. Angel of the Lord smites the Assyrians (2 Kings 19:35)
26. An angel fed Elijah in (2 Kings 19:5, 7)
27. By an angel (2 Kings 19:5–8)
28. Of Jacob, to know the name of the angel (Genesis 32:29)
29. Of Manoah, to know the name of an angel (Judges 13:17, 18)
30. Of angels, to investigate the mysteries of salvation (1 Peter 1:12)
31. Sarah, when the angels gave her the promise of a child (Genesis 18:12)
32. Of Lot, in refusing to go to the mountain, as commanded by the angels (Genesis 19:19, 20)
33. Of good angels (1 Timothy 5:21)
34. To the angels, denying her derisive laugh of unbelief (Genesis 18:15)
35. The angels (Luke 2:14)
36. Abraham to the angels (Genesis 18:1–8)
37. Lot to the angel (Genesis 19:1–11)
38. Images of angels (Colossians 2:18)
39. Reproved by an angel for not casting out the original inhabitants (Judges 2:1–5)
40. The angel Gabriel appears to Mary (at Nazareth) (Luke 1:26–38)
41. An angel appears to Joseph concerning Mary (at Nazareth) (Matthew 1:18–25)
42. Angels appear to the shepherds (in the vicinity of Bethlehem) (Luke 2:8–20)

43. Angel (Genesis 48:16; Exodus 23:20, 21)
44. Angel of his presence (Isaiah 63:9)
45. An angel appears and testifies to the innocence of his betrothed (Matthew 1:19–24)
46. Renews circumcision of the children of Israel; reestablishes the Passover; has a vision of the angel of God (Joshua 5)
47. Of angels, when Jesus was born (Luke 2:13, 14)
48. Of angels, when sinners repent (Luke 15:7, 10)
49. Received by the disposition of angels (Deuteronomy 33:2; Psalm 68:17; Acts 7:53; Galatians 3:19; Hebrews 2:2)
50. Entertains three angels, and is promised a son (Genesis 18:1–15)
51. The angel (Jude 1:9)
52. ANGELS OF THE CHURCH (Revelation 1:20; 2:1)
53. Is fed by an angel (1 Kings 19:1–8)
54. City built where Jacob wrestled with the angel (Genesis 32:31; Judges 8:8, 9, 17; 1 Kings 12:25)
55. By Jacob, his vision of angels (Genesis 28:18 with 31:13; 35:14)
56. Called "angel" (Ecclesiastes 5:6)
57. When rebuked by an angel for not expelling the Canaanites (Judges 2:1–5)
58. Hagar, commanded by an angel to return to Sarah (Sarai), her owner (Genesis 16:9)
59. Seven angels with seven trumpets (Revelation 8:2)
60. Seven angels with seven plagues (Revelation 15:6)
61. Zacharias, officiating priest, has a vision of an angel; receives promise of a son (Luke 1:5–23 with 1:57–64)
62. Of an angel (Acts 10:3)
63. Of the angel (Daniel 10)
64. Of the angel of the Lord beside the threshing floor of Ornan (1 Chronicles 21:15–18)
65. Of the ladder with ascending and descending angels (Genesis 28:12)
66. The four angels (Revelation 7:1)
67. The seventh seal and the seven angels (Revelation 8:11)
68. The four angels released from the Euphrates River (Revelation 9:14)
69. The angel that had a book (Revelation 10:1–10)
70. The angel having the everlasting gospel (Revelation 14:6,7)

71. The angel proclaiming the fall of Babylon (Revelation 14:8–13)
72. The angel reaping the harvest (Revelation 14:14–20)
73. The angel coming out of the temple (Revelation 14:17–19)
74. The angel having power over fire (Revelation 14:18)
75. The angels with the seven last plagues (Revelation 15)
76. The seven angels with the seven vials of the wrath of God (Revelation 16;)
77. The angel in the sun (Revelation 19:17–21)

Number of times the word angel *is mentioned in each book of the Bible*

Old Testament (108)

- Genesis (15)
- Exodus (6)
- Numbers (11)
- Judges (19)
- 1 Samuel (1)
- 2 Samuel (5)
- 1 Kings (3)
- 2 Kings (3)
- 1 Chronicles (7)
- 2 Chronicles (1)
- Job (1)
- Psalms (11)
- Ecclesiastes (1)
- Isaiah (2)
- Daniel (2)
- Hosea (1)
- Zechariah (19)

New Testament (175)

- Matthew (19)
- Mark (5)
- Luke (24)
- John (4)
- Acts (21)
- Romans (1)

- 1 Corinthians (4)
- 2 Corinthians (1)
- Galatians (3)
- Colossians (1)
- 2 Thessalonians (1)
- 1 Timothy (2)
- Hebrews (12)
- 1 Peter (2)
- 2 Peter (2)
- Jude (1)
- Revelation (72)

Results: 1–250

CHAPTER 14

Bible Scriptures Concerning Angels

There are 282 Bible results for the word "angel" or "angels" in the King James Version.

And the *angel* of the Lord found her by a fountain of water in the wilderness, by the fountain in the way to Shur. (Genesis 16:7)

1. And the *angel* of the Lord said unto her, return to thy mistress, and submit thyself under her hands. (Genesis 16:9)

2. And the *angel* of the Lord said unto her, I will multiply thy seed exceedingly, that it shall not be numbered for multitude. (Genesis 16:10)

3. And the *angel* of the Lord said unto her, Behold, thou art with child and shalt bear a son, and shalt call his name Ishmael, because the Lord hath heard thy affliction. (Genesis 16:11)

4. And there came two *angels* to Sodom at even; and Lot sat in the gate of Sodom: and Lot seeing them rose up to meet them; and he bowed himself with his face toward the ground. (Genesis 19:1)

5. And when the morning arose, then the *angels* hastened Lot, saying, Arise, take thy wife, and thy two daughters, which are here; lest thou be consumed in the iniquity of the city. (Genesis 19:15)

6. And God heard the voice of the lad; and the *angel* of God called to Hagar out of heaven, and said unto her, what aileth thee, Hagar? fear not; for God hath heard the voice of the lad where he is. (Genesis 21:17)

7. And the *angel* of the LORD called unto him out of heaven, and said, Abraham, Abraham: and he said, here am I. (Genesis 22:11)

8. And the *angel* of the LORD called unto Abraham out of heaven the second time. (Genesis 22:15)

9. The LORD God of heaven, which took me from my father's house, and from the land of my kindred, and which spake unto me, and that sware unto me, saying, unto thy seed will I give this land; he shall send his *angel* before thee, and thou shalt take a wife unto my son from thence. (Genesis 24:7)

10. And he said unto me, The LORD, before whom I walk, will send his *angel* with thee, and prosper thy way; and thou shalt take a wife for my son of my kindred, and of my father's house. (Genesis 24:40)

11. And he dreamed, and behold a ladder set up on the earth, and the top of it reached to heaven: and behold the *angels* of God ascending and descending on it. (Genesis 28:12)

12. And the *angel* of God spake unto me in a dream, saying, Jacob: And I said, here am I. (Genesis 31:11)

13. And Jacob went on his way, and the *angels* of God met him. (Genesis 32:1)

14. The *Angel* which redeemed me from all evil, bless the lads; and let my name be named on them, and the name of my father's Abraham and Isaac; and let them grow into a multitude in the midst of the earth. (Genesis 48:16)

15. And the *angel* of the LORD appeared unto him in a flame of fire out of the midst of a bush: and he looked, and behold,

the bush burned with fire, and the bush was not consumed. (Exodus 3:2)

16. And the *angel* of God, which went before the camp of Israel, removed, and went behind them; and the pillar of the cloud went from before their face, and stood behind them. (Exodus 14:19)

17. Behold, I send an *Angel* before thee, to keep thee in the way, and to bring thee into the place which I have prepared. (Exodus 23:20)

18. For mine *Angel* shall go before thee, and bring thee in unto the Amorites, and the Hittites, and the Perizzites, and the Canaanites, the Hivites, and the Jebusites: and I will cut them off. (Exodus 23:23)

19. Therefore, now go, lead the people unto the place of which I have spoken unto thee: behold, mine *Angel* shall go before thee: nevertheless, in the day when I visit, I will visit their sin upon them. (Exodus 32:34)

20. And I will send an *angel* before thee; and I will drive out the Canaanite, the Amorite, and the Hittite, and the Perizzite, the Hivite, and the Jebusite. (Exodus 33:2)

21. And when we cried unto the LORD, he heard our voice, and sent an *angel*, and hath brought us forth out of Egypt: and behold, we are in Kadesh, a city in the uttermost of thy border. (Numbers 20:16)

22. And God's anger was kindled because he went: and the *angel* of the LORD stood in the way for an adversary against him. Now he was riding upon his ass, and his two servants were with him. (Numbers 22:22)

23. And the ass saw the *angel* of the LORD standing in the way, and his sword drawn in his hand: and the ass turned aside out of the way and went into the field: and Balaam smote the ass, to turn her into the way. (Numbers 22:23)

24. But the *angel* of the LORD stood in a path of the vineyards, a wall being on this side, and a wall on that side. (Numbers 22:24)

25. And when the ass saw the *angel* of the LORD, she thrust herself unto the wall, and crushed Balaam's foot against the wall: and he smote her again. (Numbers 22:25)

26. And the *angel* of the LORD went further, and stood in a narrow place, where was no way to turn either to the right hand or to the left. (Numbers 22:26)

27. And when the ass saw the *angel* of the LORD, she fell down under Balaam: and Balaam's anger was kindled, and he smote the ass with a staff. (Numbers 22:27)

28. Then the LORD opened the eyes of Balaam, and he saw the *angel* of the LORD standing in the way, and his sword drawn in his hand: and he bowed down his head and fell flat on his face. (Numbers 22:31)

29. And the *angel* of the LORD said unto him, wherefore hast thou smitten thine ass these three times? behold, I went out to withstand thee, because thy way is perverse before me. (Numbers 22:32)

30. And Balaam said unto the *angel* of the LORD, I have sinned; for I knew not that thou stoodest in the way against me: now therefore, if it displeases thee, I will get me back again. (Numbers 22:34)

31. And the *angel* of the LORD said unto Balaam, go with the men: but only the word that I shall speak unto thee, that thou shalt speak. So, Balaam went with the princes of Balak. (Numbers 22:35)

32. And an *angel* of the LORD came up from Gilgal to Bochim, and said, I made you to go up out of Egypt, and have brought you unto the land which I sware unto your fathers; and I said, I will never break my covenant with you. (Judges 2:1)

33. And it came to pass, when the *angel* of the Lord spake these words unto all the children of Israel, that the people lifted their voice, and wept. (Judges 2:4)

34. Curse ye Meroz, said the *angel* of the Lord, curse ye bitterly the inhabitants thereof; because they came not to the help of the Lord, to the help of the Lord against the mighty. (Judges 5:23)

35. And there came an *angel* of the Lord, and sat under an oak which was in Ophrah, that pertained unto Joash the Abiezrite: and his son Gideon threshed wheat by the winepress, to hide it from the Midianites. (Judges 6:11)

36. And the *angel* of the Lord appeared unto him, and said unto him, The Lord is with thee, thou mighty man of valour. (Judges 6:12)

37. And the *angel* of God said unto him, Take the flesh and the unleavened cakes, and lay them upon this rock, and pour out the broth. And he did so. (Judges 6:20)

38. Then the *angel* of the Lord put forth the end of the staff that was in his hand and touched the flesh and the unleavened cakes; and there rose up fire out of the rock and consumed the flesh and the unleavened cakes. Then the *angel* of the Lord departed out of his sight. (Judges 6:21)

39. And when Gideon perceived that he was an *angel* of the Lord, Gideon said, alas, O Lord God! for because I have seen an *angel* of the Lord face to face. (Judges 6:22)

40. And the *angel* of the Lord appeared unto the woman, and said unto her, behold now, thou art barren, and bearest not: but thou shalt conceive, and bear a son. (Judges 13:3)

41. Then the woman came and told her husband, saying, A man of God came unto me, and his countenance was like the countenance of an *angel* of God, very terrible: but I asked him not whence he was, neither told he me his name. (Judges 13:6)

42.   And God hearkened to the voice of Manoah; and the *angel* of God came again unto the woman as she sat in the field: but Manoah her husband was not with her. (Judges 13:9)

43.   And the *angel* of the LORD said unto Manoah, of all that I said unto the woman let her beware. (Judges 13:13)

44.   And Manoah said unto the *angel* of the LORD, I pray thee, let us detain thee, until we shall have made ready a kid for thee. (Judges 13:15)

45.   And the *angel* of the LORD said unto Manoah, though thou detain me, I will not eat of thy bread: and if thou wilt offer a burnt offering, thou must offer it unto the LORD. For Manoah knew not that he was an *angel* of the LORD. (Judges 13:16)

46.   And Manoah said unto the *angel* of the LORD, what is thy name, that when thy sayings come to pass, we may do thee honour? (Judges 13:17)

47.   And the *angel* of the LORD said unto him, why askest thou thus after my name, seeing it is secret? (Judges 13:18)

48.   So, Manoah took a kid with a meat offering, and offered it upon a rock unto the LORD: and the *angel* did wonderously; and Manoah and his wife looked on. (Judges 13:19)

49.   For it came to pass, when the flame went up toward heaven from off the altar, that the *angel* of the LORD ascended in the flame of the altar. And Manoah and his wife looked on it and fell on their faces to the ground. (Judges 13:20)

50.   But the *angel* of the LORD did no longer appear to Manoah and to his wife. Then Manoah knew that he was an *angel* of the LORD. (Judges 13:21)

51.   And Achish answered and said to David, I know that thou art good in my sight, as an *angel* of God: notwithstanding the princes of the Philistines have said, He shall not go up with us to the battle. (1 Samuel 29:9)

52. Then thine handmaid said, the word of my lord the king shall now be comfortable: for as an *angel* of God, so is my lord the king to discern good and bad: therefore, the LORD thy God will be with thee. (2 Samuel 14:17)

53. To fetch about this form of speech hath thy servant Joab done this thing: and my lord is wise, according to the wisdom of an *angel* of God, to know all things that are in the earth. (2 Samuel 14:20)

54. And he hath slandered thy servant unto my lord the king; but my lord the king is as an *angel* of God: do therefore what is good in thine eyes. (2 Samuel 19:27)

55. And when the *angel* stretched out his hand upon Jerusalem to destroy it, the LORD repented him of the evil, and said to the *angel* that destroyed the people, it is enough: stay now thine hand. And the *angel* of the LORD was by the threshing place of Araunah the Jebusite. (2 Samuel 24:16)

56. And David spake unto the LORD when he saw the *angel* that smote the people, and said, lo, I have sinned, and I have done wickedly: but these sheep, what have they done? let thine hand, I pray thee, be against me, and against my father's house. (2 Samuel 24:17)

57. He said unto him, I am a prophet also as thou art; and an *angel* spake unto me by the word of the LORD, saying, bring him back with thee into thine house, that he may eat bread and drink water. But he lied unto him. (1 Kings 13:18)

58. And as he lay and slept under a juniper tree, behold, then an *angel* touched him, and said unto him, Arise and eat. (1 Kings 19:5)

59. And the *angel* of the LORD came again the second time, and touched him, and said, Arise and eat, because the journey is too great for thee. (1 Kings 19:7)

60. But the *angel* of the LORD said to Elijah the Tishbite, Arise, go up to meet the messengers of the king of Samaria, and

say unto them, is it not because there is not a God in Israel, that ye go to enquire of Baalzebub the god of Ekron? (2 Kings 1:3)

61. And the *angel* of the LORD said unto Elijah, go down with him be not afraid of him. And he arose and went down with him unto the king. (2 Kings 1:15)

62. And it came to pass that night, that the *angel* of the LORD went out, and smote in the camp of the Assyrians a hundred fourscore and five thousand: and when they arose early in the morning, behold, they were all dead corpses. (2 Kings 19:35)

63. Either three years' famine; or three months to be destroyed before thy foes, while that the sword of thine enemies overtaketh thee; or else three days the sword of the LORD, even the pestilence, in the land, and the *angel* of the LORD destroying throughout all the coasts of Israel. Now therefore advise thyself what word I shall bring again to him that sent me. (1 Chronicles 21:12)

64. And God sent an *angel* unto Jerusalem to destroy it: and as he was destroying, the LORD beheld, and he repented him of the evil, and said to the *angel* that destroyed, it is enough, stay now thine hand. And the *angel* of the LORD stood by the threshing floor of Ornan the Jebusite. (1 Chronicles 21:15)

65. And David lifted up his eyes and saw the *angel* of the LORD stand between the earth and the heaven, having a drawn sword in his hand stretched out over Jerusalem. Then David and the elders of Israel, who were clothed in sackcloth, fell upon their faces. (1 Chronicles 21:16)

66. Then the *angel* of the LORD commanded Gad to say to David, that David should go up, and set up an altar unto the LORD in the threshing floor of Ornan the Jebusite. (1 Chronicles 21:18)

67. And Ornan turned back and saw the *angel*; and his four sons with him hid themselves. Now Ornan was threshing wheat. (1 Chronicles 21:20)

68. And the LORD commanded the *angel*; and he put up his sword again into the sheath thereof. (1 Chronicles 21:27)

69. But David could not go before it to enquire of God: for he was afraid because of the sword of the *angel* of the LORD. (1 Chronicles 21:30)

70. And the LORD sent an *angel*, which cut off all the mighty men of valour, and the leaders and captains in the camp of the king of Assyria. So, he returned with shame of face to his own land. And when he was come into the house of his god, they that came forth of his own bowels slew him there with the sword. (2 Chronicles 32:21)

71. Behold, he put no trust in his servants; and his *angels* he charged with folly. (Job 4:18)

72. For thou hast made him a little lower than the *angels*, and hast crowned him with glory and honour. (Psalm 8:5)

73. The *angel* of the LORD encampeth round about them that fear him, and delivereth them. (Psalm 34:7)

74. Let them be as chaff before the wind: and let the *angel* of the LORD chase them. (Psalm 35:5)

75. Let their way be dark and slippery: and let the *angel* of the LORD persecute them. (Psalm 35:6)

76. The chariots of God are twenty thousand, even thousands of *angels*: the Lord is among them, as in Sinai, in the holy place. (Psalm 68:17)

77. Man did eat *angels'* food: he sent them meat to the full. (Psalm 78:25)

78. He cast upon them the fierceness of his anger, wrath, and indignation, and trouble, by sending evil *angels* among them. (Psalm 78:49)

79. For he shall give his *angels* charge over thee, to keep thee in all thy ways. (Psalm 91:11)

80. Bless the LORD, ye his *angels*, that excel in strength, that do his commandments, hearkening unto the voice of his word. (Psalm 103:20)

81. Who maketh his *angels'* spirits; his ministers a flaming fire. (Psalm 104:4)

82. Praise ye him, all his *angels*: praise ye him, all his hosts. (Psalm 148:2)

83. Suffer not thy mouth to cause thy flesh to sin; neither say thou before the *angel*, that it was an error: wherefore should God be angry at thy voice, and destroy the work of thine hands? (Ecclesiastes 5:6)

84. Then the angel of the LORD went forth and smote in the camp of the Assyrians a hundred and fourscore and five thousand: and when they arose early in the morning, behold, they were all dead corpses. (Isaiah 37:36)

85. In all their affliction he was afflicted, and the *angel* of his presence saved them: in his love and in his pity, he redeemed them; and he bare them, and carried them all the days of old. (Isaiah 63:9)

86. Then Nebuchadnezzar spake, and said, blessed be the God of Shadrach, Meshach, and Abednego, who hath sent his *angel*, and delivered his servants that trusted in him, and have changed the king's word, and yielded their bodies, that they might not serve nor worship any god, except their own God. (Daniel 3:28)

87. My God hath sent his *angel*, and hath shut the lions' mouths, that they have not hurt me: forasmuch as before him innocence was found in me; and, before thee, O king, have I done no hurt. (Daniel 6:22)

88. Yea, he had power over the *angel*, and prevailed: he wept, and made supplication unto him: he found him in Bethel, and there he spake with us. (Hosea 12:4)

89. Then said I, O my lord, what are these? And the *angel* that talked with me said unto me, I will shew thee what these be. 9Zechariah 1:9)

90. And they answered the *angel* of the Lord that stood among the myrtle trees, and said, we have walked to and fro through the earth, and behold, all the earth sitteth still, and is at rest. (Zechariah 1:11)

91. Then the *angel* of the Lord answered and said, O Lord of hosts, how long wilt thou not have mercy on Jerusalem and on the cities of Judah, against which thou hast had indignation these threescore and ten years? (Zechariah 1:12)

92. And the Lord answered the *angel* that talked with me with good words and comfortable words. (Zechariah 1:13)

93. So, the *angel* that communed with me said unto me, cry thou, saying, thus saith the Lord of hosts; I am jealous for Jerusalem and for Zion with a great jealousy. (Zechariah 1:14)

94. And I said unto the *angel* that talked with me, what be these? And he answered me, these are the horns which have scattered Judah, Israel, and Jerusalem. (Zechariah 1:19)

95. And behold, the *angel* that talked with me went forth, and another *angel* went out to meet him. (Zechariah 2:3)

96. And he shewed me Joshua the high priest standing before the *angel* of the Lord, and Satan standing at his right hand to resist him. (Zechariah 3:1)

97. Now Joshua was clothed with filthy garments and stood before the *angel*. (Zechariah 3:3)

98. And I said, let them set a fair mitre upon his head. So, they set a fair mitre upon his head, and clothed him with garments. And the *angel* of the Lord stood by. (Zechariah 3:5)

99. And the *angel* of the Lord protested unto Joshua, saying. (Zechariah 3:6)

100. And the *angel* that talked with me came again, and waked me, as a man that is wakened out of his sleep. (Zechariah 4:1)

101. So, I answered and spake to the *angel* that talked with me, saying, what are these, my lord? (Zechariah 4:4)

102. Then the *angel* that talked with me answered and said unto me, Knowest thou not what these be? And I said, No, my lord. (Zechariah 4:5)

103. Then the *angel* that talked with me went forth, and said unto me, Lift up now thine eyes, and see what is this that goeth forth. (Zechariah 5:5)

104. Then said I to the *angel* that talked with me, whither do these bear the ephah? (Zechariah 5:10)

105. Then I answered and said unto the *angel* that talked with me, what are these, my lord? (Zechariah 6:4)

106. And the *angel* answered and said unto me, these are the four spirits of the heavens, which go forth from standing before the LORD of all the earth. (Zechariah 6:5)

107. In that day shall the LORD defend the inhabitants of Jerusalem; and he that is feeble among them at that day shall be as David; and the house of David shall be as God, as the *angel* of the LORD before them. (Zechariah 12:8)

108. But while he thought on these things, behold, the *angel* of the LORD appeared unto him in a dream, saying, Joseph, thou son of David, fear not to take unto the Mary thy wife: for that which is conceived in her is of the Holy Ghost. (Matthew 1:20)

109. Then Joseph being raised from sleep did as the *angel* of the Lord had bidden him, and took unto him his wife. (Matthew 1:24)

110. And when they were departed, behold, the *angel* of the Lord appeareth to Joseph in a dream, saying, Arise, and take the young child and his mother, and flee into Egypt,

and be thou there until I bring thee word: for Herod will seek the young child to destroy him. (Matthew 2:13)

111. But when Herod was dead, behold, an *angel* of the Lord appeareth in a dream to Joseph in Egypt. (Matthew 2:19)

112. And saith unto him, if thou be the Son of God, cast thyself down: for it is written, He shall give his *angels* charge concerning thee: and in their hands they shall bear thee up, lest at any time thou dash thy foot against a stone. (Matthew 4:6)

113. Then the devil leaveth him, and behold, *angels* came and ministered unto him. (Matthew 4:11)

114. The enemy that sowed them is the devil; the harvest is the end of the world; and the reapers are the *angels*. (Matthew 13:39)

115. The Son of man shall send forth his *angels*, and they shall gather out of his kingdom all things that offend, and them which do iniquity. (Matthew 13:41)

116. So shall it be at the end of the world: the *angels* shall come forth, and sever the wicked from among the just. (Matthew 13:49)

117. For the Son of man shall come in the glory of his Father with his *angels*; and then he shall reward every man according to his works. (Matthew 16:27)

118. Take heed that ye despise not one of these little ones; for I say unto you, that in heaven their *angels* do always behold the face of my Father which is in heaven. (Matthew 18:10)

119. For in the resurrection, they neither marry, nor are given in marriage, but are as the *angels* of God in heaven. (Matthew 22:30)

120. And he shall send his *angels* with a great sound of a trumpet, and they shall gather his elect from the four winds, from one end of heaven to the other. (Matthew 24:31)

121. But of that day and hour knoweth no man, no, not the *angels* of heaven, but my Father only. (Matthew 24:36)

122. When the Son of man shall come in his glory, and all the holy *angels* with him, then shall he sit upon the throne of his glory. (Matthew 25:31)

123. Then shall he say also unto them on the left hand, depart from me, ye cursed, into everlasting fire, prepared for the devil and his *angels*. (Matthew 25:41)

124. Thinkest thou that I cannot now pray to my Father, and he shall presently give me more than twelve legions of *angels*? (Matthew 26:53)

125. And behold, there was a great earthquake: for the *angel* of the Lord descended from heaven and came and rolled back the stone from the door and sat upon it. (Matthew 28:2)

126. And the *angel* answered and said unto the women, Fear not ye: for I know that ye seek Jesus, which was crucified. (Matthew 28:5)

127. And he was there in the wilderness forty days, tempted of Satan; and was with the wild beasts; and the *angels* ministered unto him. (Mark 1:13)

128. Whosoever therefore shall be ashamed of me and of my words in this adulterous and sinful generation; of him also shall the Son of man be ashamed, when he cometh in the glory of his Father with the holy *angels*. (Mark 8:38)

129. For when they shall rise from the dead, they neither marry, nor are given in marriage; but are as the *angels* which are in heaven. (Mark 12:25)

130. And then shall he send his *angels* and shall gather together his elect from the four winds, from the uttermost part of the earth to the uttermost part of heaven. (Mark 13:27)

131. But of that day and that hour knoweth no man, no, not the *angels* which are in heaven, neither the Son, but the Father. (Mark 13:32)

132. And there appeared unto him an *angel* of the Lord standing on the right side of the altar of incense. (Luke 1:11)

133. But the *angel* said unto him, Fear not, Zacharias: for thy prayer is heard; and thy wife Elisabeth shall bear thee a son, and thou shalt call his name John. (Luke 1:130

134. And Zacharias said unto the *angel*, whereby shall I know this? for I am an old man, and my wife well stricken in years. (Luke 1:18)

135. And the *angel* answering said unto him, I am Gabriel, that stand in the presence of God; and am sent to speak unto thee, and to shew thee these glad tidings. (Luke 1:19)

136. And in the sixth month the *angel* Gabriel was sent from God unto a city of Galilee, named Nazareth. (Luke 1:260

137. And the *angel* came in unto her, and said, Hail, thou that art highly favoured, the Lord is with thee: blessed art thou among women. (Luke 1:28)

138. And the *angel* said unto her, Fear not, Mary: for thou hast found favour with God. (Luke 1:30)

139. Then said Mary unto the *angel*, how shall this be, seeing I know not a man? (Luke 1:34)

140. And the *angel* answered and said unto her, The Holy Ghost shall come upon thee, and the power of the Highest shall overshadow thee: therefore, also that holy thing which shall be born of thee shall be called the Son of God. (Luke 1:35)

141. And Mary said, Behold the handmaid of the Lord; be it unto me according to thy word. And the *angel* departed from her. (Luke 1:38)

142. And, lo, the *angel* of the Lord came upon them, and the glory of the Lord shone round about them: and they were sore afraid. (Luke 2:9)

143. And the *angel* said unto them, Fear not: for, behold, I bring you good tidings of great joy, which shall be to all people. (Luke 2:10)

144. And suddenly there was with the *angel* a multitude of the heavenly host praising God, and saying. (Luke 2:13)

145. And it came to pass, as the *angels* were gone away from them into heaven, the shepherds said one to another, let us now go even unto Bethlehem, and see this thing, which is come to pass, which the Lord hath made known unto us. (Luke 2:15)

146. And when eight days were accomplished for the circumcising of the child, his name was called Jesus, which was so named of the *angel* before he was conceived in the womb. (Luke 2:21)

147. For it is written, He shall give his angels charge over thee, to keep thee. (Luke 4:10)

148. For whosoever shall be ashamed of me and of my words, of him shall the Son of man be ashamed, when he shall come in his own glory, and in his Father's, and of the holy angels. (Luke 9:26)

149. Also, I say unto you, whosoever shall confess me before men, him shall the Son of man also confess before the angels of God. (Luke 12:8)

150. But he that denieth me before men shall be denied before the angels of God. (Luke 12:9)

151. Likewise, I say unto you, there is joy in the presence of the angels of God over one sinner that repenteth. (Luke 15:10)

152. And it came to pass, that the beggar died, and was carried by the angels into Abraham's bosom: the rich man also died and was buried. (Luke 16:22)

153. Neither can they die any more: for they are equal unto the angels; and are the children of God, being the children of the resurrection. (Luke 20:36)

154. And there appeared an angel unto him from heaven, strengthening him. (Luke 22:43)

155. And when they found not his body, they came, saying, that they had also seen a vision of angels, which said that he was alive. (Luke 24:23)

156. And he saith unto him, Verily, verily, I say unto you, Hereafter ye shall see heaven open, and the angels of God ascending and descending upon the Son of man. (John 1:51)

157. For an angel went down at a certain season into the pool and troubled the water: whosoever then first after the troubling of the water stepped in was made whole of whatsoever disease he had. (John 5:4)

158. The people, therefore, that stood by, and heard it, said that it thundered: others said, An angel spake to him. (John 12:29)

159. And seeth two angels in white sitting, the one at the head, and the other at the feet, where the body of Jesus had lain. (John 20:12)

160. But the angel of the Lord by night opened the prison doors, and brought them forth, and said. (Acts 5:19)

161. And all that sat in the council, looking stedfastly on him, saw his face as it had been the face of an angel. (Acts 6:15)

162. And when forty years were expired, there appeared to him in the wilderness of mount Sina an angel of the Lord in a flame of fire in a bush. (Acts 7:30)

163. This Moses whom they refused, saying, who made thee a ruler and a judge? the same did God send to be a ruler and

a deliverer by the hand of the angel which appeared to him in the bush. (Acts 7:35)

164. This is he, that was in the church in the wilderness with the angel which spake to him in the mount Sina, and with our fathers: who received the lively oracles to give unto us. (Acts 7:38)

165. Who have received the law by the disposition of angels, and have not kept it? (Acts 7:53)

166. And the angel of the Lord spake unto Philip, saying, Arise, and go toward the south unto the way that goeth down from Jerusalem unto Gaza, which is desert. (Acts 8:26)

167. He saw in a vision evidently about the ninth hour of the day an angel of God coming into him, and saying unto him, Cornelius. (Acts 10:3)

168. And when the angel which spake unto Cornelius was departed, he called two of his household servants, and a devout soldier of them that waited on him continually. (Acts 10:7)

169. And they said, Cornelius the centurion, a just man, and one that feareth God, and of good report among all the nation of the Jews, was warned from God by a holy angel to send for thee into his house, and to hear words of thee. (Acts 10:22)

170. And he shewed us how he had seen an angel in his house, which stood and said unto him, send men to Joppa, and call for Simon, whose surname is Peter. (Acts 11:13)

171. And behold, the angel of the Lord came upon him, and a light shined in the prison: and he smote Peter on the side, and raised him up, saying, Arise up quickly. And his chains fell off from his hands. (Acts 12:7)

172. And the angel said unto him, gird thyself, and bind on thy sandals. And so, he did. And he saith unto him, cast thy garment about thee, and follow me. (Acts 12:8)

173. And he went out and followed him; and wist not that it was true which was done by the angel; but thought he saw a vision. (Acts 12:9)

174. When they were past the first and the second ward, they came unto the iron gate that leadeth unto the city; which opened to them of his own accord: and they went out and passed on through one street; and forthwith the angel departed from him. (Acts 12:10)

175. And when Peter was come to himself, he said, Now I know of a surety, that the LORD hath sent his angel, and hath delivered me out of the hand of Herod, and from all the expectation of the people of the Jews. (Acts 12:11)

176. And they said unto her, Thou art mad. But she constantly affirmed that it was even so. Then said they, it is his angel. (Acts 12:15)

177. And immediately the angel of the Lord smote him because he gave not God the glory: and he was eaten of worms and gave up the ghost. (Acts 12:23)

178. For the Sadducees say that there is no resurrection, neither angel, nor spirit: but the Pharisees confess both. (Acts 23:8)

179. And there arose a great cry: and the scribes that were of the Pharisees' part arose, and strove, saying, we find no evil in this man: but if a spirit or an angel hath spoken to him, let us not fight against God. (Acts 23:9)

180. For there stood by me this night the angel of God, whose I am, and whom I serve. (Acts 27:23)

181. For I am persuaded, that neither death, nor life, nor angels, nor principalities, nor powers, nor things present, nor things to come. (Romans 8:38)

182. For I think that God hath set forth us the apostles last, as it were appointed to death: for we are made a spectacle unto the world, and to angels, and to men. (1 Corinthians 4:9)

183. Know ye not that we shall judge angels? how much more things that pertain to this life? (1 Corinthians 6:3)

184. For this cause ought the woman to have power on her head because of the angels. 91 Corinthians 11:10)

185. Though I speak with the tongues of men and of angels, and have not charity, I am become as sounding brass, or a tinkling cymbal. (1 Corinthians 13:1)

186. And no marvel; for Satan himself is transformed into an angel of light. (2 Corinthians 11:14)

187. But though we, or an angel from heaven, preach any other gospel unto you than that which we have preached unto you, let him be accursed. (Galatians 1:8)

188. Wherefore then serveth the law? It was added because of transgressions, till the seed should come to whom the promise was made; and it was ordained by angels in the hand of a mediator. (Galatians 3:19)

189. And my temptation which was in my flesh ye despised not, nor rejected; but received me as an angel of God, even as Christ Jesus. (Galatians 4:14)

190. Let no man beguile you of your reward in a voluntary humility and worshipping of angels, intruding into those things which he hath not seen, vainly puffed up by his fleshly mind. (Colossians 2:18)

191. And to you who are troubled rest with us, when the Lord Jesus shall be revealed from heaven with his mighty angels. (2 Thessalonians 1:7)

192. And without controversy great is the mystery of godliness: God was manifest in the flesh, justified in the Spirit, seen of angels, preached unto the Gentiles, believed on in the world, received up into glory. (1 Timothy 3:16)

193. I charge thee before God, and the Lord Jesus Christ, and the elect angels, that thou observe these things without preferring one before another, doing nothing by partiality. (1 Timothy 5:21)

194. Being made so much better than the angels, as he hath by inheritance obtained a more excellent name than they. (Hebrews 1:4)

195. For unto which of the angels said he at any time, thou art my Son, this day have I begotten thee? And again, I will be to him a father, and he shall be to me a Son? (Hebrews 1:5)

196. And again, when he bringeth in the firstbegotten into the world, he saith, and let all the angels of God worship him. (Hebrews 1:6)

197. And of the angels he saith, Who maketh his angels' spirits, and his ministers a flame of fire. (Hebrews 1:70

198. But to which of the angels said he at any time, sit on my right hand, until I make thine enemies thy footstool? (Hebrews 1:13)

199. For if the word spoken by angels was stedfast, and every transgression and disobedience received a just recompence of reward. (Hebrews 2:2)

200. For unto the angels hath he not put in subjection the world to come, whereof we speak. (Hebrews 2:5)

201. Thou madest him a little lower than the angels; thou crownedst him with glory and honour, and didst set him over the works of thy hands. (Hebrews 2:7)

202. But we see Jesus, who was made a little lower than the angels for the suffering of death, crowned with glory and honour; that he by the grace of God should taste death for every man. (Hebrews 2:9)

203. For verily he took not on him the nature of angels; but he took on him the seed of Abraham. (Hebrews 2:16)

204. But ye are come unto mount Sion, and unto the city of the living God, the heavenly Jerusalem, and to an innumerable company of angels. (Hebrews 12:22)

205. Be not forgetful to entertain strangers: for thereby some have entertained angels unawares. (Hebrews 13:2)

206. Unto whom it was revealed, that not unto themselves, but unto us they did minister the things, which are now reported unto you by them that have preached the gospel unto you with the Holy Ghost sent down from heaven, which things the angels desire to look into. (1 Peter 1:12)

207. Who is gone into heaven, and is on the right hand of God; angels and authorities and powers being made subject unto him? (1 Peter 3:22)

208. For if God spared not the angels that sinned, but cast them down to hell, and delivered them into chains of darkness, to be reserved unto judgment. (2 Peter 2:4)

209. Whereas angels, who are greater in power and might, bring not railing accusation against them before the Lord. (2 Peter 2:11)

210. And the angels who kept not their first estate, but left their own habitation, he hath reserved in everlasting chains under darkness unto the judgment of the great day. (Jude 1:6)

211. The Revelation of Jesus Christ, which God gave unto him, to shew unto his servants' things which must shortly come to pass; and he sent and signified it by his angel unto his servant John. (Revelation 1:1)

212. The mystery of the seven stars which thou sawest in my right hand, and the seven golden candlesticks. The seven stars are the angels of the seven churches: and the seven candlesticks which thou sawest are the seven churches. (Revelation 1:20)

213. Unto the angel of the church of Ephesus write, These things saith he that holdeth the seven stars in his right hand, who

walketh in the midst of the seven golden candlesticks. (Revelation 2:1)

214. And unto the angel of the church in Smyrna write, these things saith the first and the last, which was dead, and is alive. (Revelation 2:8)

215. And to the angel of the church in Pergamos write; These things saith he which hath the sharp sword with two edges. (Revelation 2:12)

216. And unto the angel of the church in Thyatira write, these things saith the Son of God, who hath his eyes like unto a flame of fire, and his feet are like fine brass. (Revelation 2:18)

217. And unto the angel of the church in Sardis write, these things saith he that hath the seven Spirits of God, and the seven stars; I know thy works, that thou hast a name that thou livest, and art dead. (Revelation 3:1)

218. He that overcometh, the same shall be clothed in white raiment; and I will not blot out his name out of the book of life, but I will confess his name before my Father, and before his angels. (Revelation 3:5)

219. And to the angel of the church in Philadelphia write, these things saith he that is holy, he that is true, he that hath the key of David, he that openeth, and no man shutteth; and shutteth, and no man openeth. (Revelation 3:7)

220. And unto the angel of the church of the Laodiceans write; These things saith the Amen, the faithful and true witness, the beginning of the creation of God. (Revelation 3:14)

221. And I saw a strong angel proclaiming with a loud voice, who is worthy to open the book, and to lose the seals thereof? (Revelation 5:2)

222. And I beheld, and I heard the voice of many angels round about the throne and the beasts and the elders: and the

number of them was ten thousand times ten thousand, and thousands of thousands. (Revelation 5:11)

223. And after these things I saw four angels standing on the four corners of the earth, holding the four winds of the earth, that the wind should not blow on the earth, nor on the sea, nor on any tree. (Revelation 7:1)

224. And I saw another angel ascending from the east, having the seal of the living God: and he cried with a loud voice to the four angels, to whom it was given to hurt the earth and the sea. (Revelation 7:2)

225. And all the angels stood round about the throne, and about the elders and the four beasts, and fell before the throne on their faces, and worshipped God. (Revelation 7:11)

226. And I saw the seven angels which stood before God; and to them were given seven trumpets. (Revelation 8:2)

227. And another angel came and stood at the altar, having a golden censer; and there was given unto him much incense, that he should offer it with the prayers of all saints upon the golden altar which was before the throne. (Revelation 8:3)

228. And the smoke of the incense, which came with the prayers of the saints, ascended up before God out of the angel's hand. (Revelation 8:4)

229. And the angel took the censer, and filled it with fire of the altar, and cast it into the earth: and there were voices, and thunderings, and lightnings, and an earthquake. (Revelation 8:5)

230. And the seven angels who had the seven trumpets prepared themselves to sound. (Revelation 8:6)

231. The first angel sounded, and there followed hail and fire mingled with blood, and they were cast upon the earth: and the third part of trees was burnt up, and all green grass was burnt up. (Revelation 8:7)

232. And the second angel sounded, and as it were a great mountain burning with fire was cast into the sea: and the third part of the sea became blood. (Revelation 8:8)

233. And the third angel sounded, and there fell a great star from heaven, burning as it were a lamp, and it fell upon the third part of the rivers, and upon the fountains of waters. (Revelation 8:10)

234. And the fourth angel sounded, and the third part of the sun was smitten, and the third part of the moon, and the third part of the stars; so, as the third part of them was darkened, and the day shone not for a third part of it, and the night likewise. (Revelation 8:12)

235. And I beheld and heard an angel flying through the midst of heaven, saying with a loud voice, Woe, woe, woe, to the inhabiters of the earth by reason of the other voices of the trumpet of the three angels, which are yet to sound! (Revelation 8:13)

236. And the fifth angel sounded, and I saw a star fall from heaven unto the earth: and to him was given the key to the bottomless pit. (Revelation 9:1)

237. And they had a king over them, which is the angel of the bottomless pit, whose name in the Hebrew tongue is Abaddon, but in the Greek tongue hath his name Apollyon. (Revelation 9:11)

238. And the sixth angel sounded, and I heard a voice from the four horns of the golden altar, which is before God. (Revelation 9:13)

239. Saying to the sixth angel which had the trumpet, Loose the four angels which are bound in the great river Euphrates. (Revelation 9:14)

240. And the four angels were loosed, which were prepared for an hour, and a day, and a month, and a year, for to slay the third part of men. (Revelation 9:15)

241. And I saw another mighty angel come down from heaven, clothed with a cloud: and a rainbow was upon his head, and his face was as it were the sun, and his feet as pillars of fire. (Revelation 10:1)

242. And the angel who I saw stand upon the sea and upon the earth lifted up his hand to heaven. (Revelation 10:5)

243. But in the days of the voice of the seventh angel, when he shall begin to sound, the mystery of God should be finished, as he hath declared to his servants the prophets. (Revelation 10:7)

244. And the voice which I heard from heaven spake unto me again, and said, Go and take the little book which is open in the hand of the angel which standeth upon the sea and upon the earth. (Revelation 10:8)

245. And I went unto the angel, and said unto him, Give me the little book. And he said unto me, take it, and eat it up; and it shall make thy belly bitter, but it shall be in thy mouth sweet as honey. (Revelation 10:9)

246. And I took the little book out of the angel's hand and ate it up; and it was in my mouth sweet as honey: and as soon as I had eaten it, my belly was bitter. (Revelation 10:10)

247. And there was given me a reed like unto a rod: and the angel stood, saying, Rise, and measure the temple of God, and the altar, and them that worship therein. (Revelation 11:1)

248. And the seventh angel sounded; and there were great voices in heaven, saying, the kingdoms of this world are become the kingdoms of our Lord, and of his Christ; and he shall reign for ever and ever. (Revelation 11:15)

249. And there was war in heaven: Michael and his angels fought against the dragon; and the dragon fought and his angels. (Revelation 12:7)

250. And the great dragon was cast out, that old serpent, called the Devil, and Satan, which deceiveth the whole world: he was cast out into the earth, and his angels were cast out with him. (Revelation 12:9)

251. And I saw another angel fly in the midst of heaven, having the everlasting gospel to preach unto them that dwell on the earth, and to every nation, and kindred, and tongue, and people. (Revelation 14:6)

252. And there followed another angel, saying, Babylon is fallen, is fallen, that great city, because she made all nations drink of the wine of the wrath of her fornication. (Revelation 14:8)

253. And the third angel followed them, saying with a loud voice, if any man worship the beast and his image, and receive his mark in his forehead, or in his hand. (Revelation 14:9)

254. The same shall drink of the wine of the wrath of God, which is poured out without mixture into the cup of his indignation; and he shall be tormented with fire and brimstone in the presence of the holy angels, and in the presence of the Lamb. (Revelation 14:10)

255. And another angel came out of the temple, crying with a loud voice to him that sat on the cloud, thrust in thy sickle, and reap for the time is come for thee to reap; for the harvest of the earth is ripe. (Revelation 14:15)

256. And another angel came out of the temple, which is in heaven, he also having a sharp sickle. (Revelation 14:17)

257. And another angel came out from the altar, which had power over fire; and cried with a loud cry to him that had the sharp sickle, saying, thrust in thy sharp sickle, and gather the clusters of the vine of the earth; for her grapes are fully ripe. (Revelation 14:18)

258. And the angel thrust in his sickle into the earth, and gathered the vine of the earth, and cast it into the great winepress of the wrath of God. (Revelation 14:19)

259. And I saw another sign in heaven, great and marvellous, seven *angels* having the seven last plagues; for in them is filled up the wrath of God. (Revelation 15:1)

260. And the seven angels came out of the temple, having the seven plagues, clothed in pure and white linen, and having their breasts girded with golden girdles. (Revelation 15:6)

261. And one of the four beasts gave unto the seven angels seven golden vials full of the wrath of God, who liveth for ever and ever. (Revelation 15:7)

262. And the temple was filled with smoke from the glory of God, and from his power; and no man was able to enter the temple, till the seven plagues of the seven angels were fulfilled. (Revelation 15:8)

263. And I heard a great voice out of the temple saying to the seven angels, go your ways, and pour out the vials of the wrath of God upon the earth. (Revelation 16:1)

264. And the second angel poured out his vial upon the sea; and it became as the blood of a dead man: and every living soul died in the sea. (Revelation 16:3)

265. And the third angel poured out his vial upon the rivers and fountains of waters; and they became blood. (Revelation 16:4)

266. And I heard the angel of the waters say, thou art righteous, O Lord, which art, and wast, and shalt be, because thou hast judged thus. (Revelation 16:5)

267. And the fourth angel poured out his vial upon the sun; and power was given unto him to scorch men with fire. (Revelation 16:8)

268. And the fifth angel poured out his vial upon the seat of the beast; and his kingdom was full of darkness; and they gnawed their tongues for pain. (Revelation 16:10)

269. And the sixth angel poured out his vial upon the great river Euphrates; and the water thereof was dried up, that the way of the kings of the east might be prepared. (Revelation 16:12)

270. And the seventh angel poured out his vial into the air; and there came a great voice out of the temple of heaven, from the throne, saying, it is done. (Revelation 16:17)

271. And there came one of the seven angels which had the seven vials, and talked with me, saying unto me, come hither; I will shew unto thee the judgment of the great whore that sitteth upon many waters. (Revelation 17:1)

272. And the angel said unto me, wherefore didst thou marvel? I will tell thee the mystery of the woman, and of the beast that carrieth her, which hath the seven heads and ten horns. (Revelation 17:7)

273. And after these things I saw another angel come down from heaven, having great power; and the earth was lightened with his glory. (Revelation 18:1)

274. And a mighty angel took up a stone like a great millstone, and cast it into the sea, saying, thus with violence shall that great city Babylon be thrown down, and shall be found no more at all. (Revelation 18:21)

275. And I saw an angel standing in the sun; and he cried with a loud voice, saying to all the fowls that fly in the midst of heaven, Come and gather yourselves together unto the supper of the great God. (Revelation 19:17)

276. And I saw an angel come down from heaven, having the key to the bottomless pit and a great chain in his hand. (Revelation 20:1)

277. And there came unto me one of the seven angels which had the seven vials full of the seven last plagues, and talked with me, saying, come hither, I will shew thee the bride, the Lamb's wife. (Revelation 21:9)

278. And had a wall great and high, and had twelve gates, and at the gates twelve angels, and names written thereon, which are the names of the twelve tribes of the children of Israel. (Revelation 21:12)

279. And he measured the wall thereof, a hundred and forty and four cubits, according to the measure of a man, that is, of the angel. (Revelation 21:17)

280. And he said unto me, these sayings are faithful and true: and the Lord God of the holy prophets sent his angel to shew unto his servants the things which must shortly be done. (Revelation 22:6)

281. And I John saw these things and heard them. And when I had heard and seen, I fell down to worship before the feet of the angel which shewed me these things. (Revelation 22:8)

282. I Jesus have sent mine angel to testify unto you these things in the churches. I am the root and the offspring of David, and the bright and morning star. (Revelation 22:16)

If you have completed this study of the *Doctrine of Angels*, it is my prayer you have a better understand of who angels are, what their purpose is, and why God created them. Angels are all around us. We should believe and expect them to work on our behalf according to the Word of God. I believe I have written this study based on the Word of God and pray it will and has benefited you and your study of this wonderful gift God has given us.

My friend Rev. Timothy Williams has authored a wonderful book titled, "Angels Are Among Us". It is the most balanced book on the doctrine of angels I have ever read. I have read a lot of bizarre unscriptural books and articles concerning angels. Tim has dug through the scriptures and gives you a true Biblical approach to the understanding of angels, where they come from, what their assignment on the earth is, and how we can use them in our daily lifestyle. Get this book, read it, study it, and its principles will change your life.

Rev. David Copeland
"Revival Now International Ministries",
International minister, teacher, and missionary.

It is with immense pleasure and confidence that I recommend this study on the Doctrine of Angels, authored by Rev. Timothy Williams. As someone who has been actively involved in ministry for over 35 years, I have read and studied books and articles on this subject matter; but this is by far the most complete, comprehensive, and balanced presentation I have seen. I know you will find it informative, helpful, and encouraging as you discover the reality of angels and the authority, diversity and the divine assistance that is present and operative in the Unseen Realm.

Rev. Marty Blackwelder
International traveling minister and teacher.
Traveled 11 years with Brother Kenneth Hagin
on the crusade team.
Associate Pastor at Rhema Bible Church 5 years
Instructor at Rhema Bible School for 5 years.

There are people you meet in life that are temporary, but there are also people who are divine appointments and become friends for life. Rev. Tim Williams is the latter. I highly recommend this book which is full of biblical knowledge about angels and how they operate in our lives today. May the Holy Spirit enlighten you as you read and study this book. By reading Tim's book on angels, you will become one who genuinely believes in angels and allows them to operate in your life. Rev. Tim Williams has been a missionary for 28 years, I have been associated and friends with him for 18 years.

Rev. Mike Merritt
Associate Pastor at Grace Christian Fellowship,
Little River, SC
Retired Pastor of Abundant Life Church
in Newnan, Ga.

ABOUT THE AUTHOR

Timothy R Williams has been a missionary for twenty-eight years. He has traveled extensively in Haiti; Guyana, South America; Nicaragua; Kenya, Africa; and the Southeastern United States. In 1995, while on his first mission trip to Haiti, God spoke to him and gave him his assignment and purpose in life, "to go to the nations, preach the gospel, teach faith, lay hands on the sick, and operate as the Holy Spirit directed." His focus has been to teach and equip others to fulfill their assignments and purpose in life, to preach the gospel so the lost would be saved. He has been actively involved with orphanages in each of the four countries he has been called to. He has a profound revelation of the Word of God. He teaches and preaches with simplicity and clarity with an emphasis on God's love. His teaching and preaching teach people how to live by faith and walk in divine healing.

He graduated from Rhema Bible Training Center in 2002 and Victory World Missions in 2003. At thirty-nine years old, he gave up a successful sales career to follow the plan that God had given him. He moved his family to Tulsa, Oklahoma, where he lived for the next three years training and studying God's Word. At the time of this printing, he and his wife, Tammy, have been married for forty-five years. They have three children and nine grandchildren. They currently live in North Florida that has allowed for easy travel to the different destinations that God choses to send him. His ministry name is Healing Hands International Ministries Inc., and his ministry motto is, "Lord, send me." He has always been willing to go where others would not go and do what others were not willing to do. God specifically told him in 1995 that he was to be an itinerant missionary, traveling back and forth from the US, and he would not live on the mission field.